TEACH YOUR KIDS ABOUT

JESUS

TEACH YOUR KIDS ABOUT

JESUS

Lessons for Kids about the Life, Teachings, and Ministry of Jesus Christ

JOSEPH HENSON

Published by Gainsborough Press

Editorial Consultant: William Linney
Editorial Consultant: Michael Garnier
Editorial Assistant: Geraldine Linney

ISBN: 978-0-9825166-0-7

Library of Congress Control Number: 2010902610

CONTENTS

Part III: The Ministry of Jesus   35

Part IV: The Miracles of Jesus   51

Part V: Jesus the Great Teacher   69

Part VI: Jesus and the Kingdom of God 89

Part VII: Jesus and Life in the Kingdom 101

Part VIII: Jesus the Savior (Passion Week) 129

Answer Key 159

PREFACE

The book you are holding represents my life's passion: to know Jesus and to make him known to others. The harsh realities of our times only serve to fuel that passion. For example, our culture is being hammered by the dogma that human life is the result of an aimless and unguided process—a cosmic accident—and that life is ultimately without meaning or purpose. The illusion of materialism is leaving people empty and hopeless. Even worse, the person and work of Christ is being redefined and undermined as you read these words. As a father, I feel a special burden to make sure that my children and others in their generation do not fall prey to these destructive ideas. Rather, it is my hope that they come to know the One who gives humanity ultimate meaning and purpose—and I know I am not alone.

I believe many parents want to introduce their children to Jesus, but they feel intimidated by the size and seeming difficulty of the Bible itself. This book is designed to address that problem. It is designed to equip and empower parents to teach their kids about Jesus.

Each of the eight large sections of *Teach Your Kids About Jesus* explores one of the main themes of the life and ministry of Christ. The individual lessons within each section explore important theological truths in a simple, straightforward manner that kids can readily understand. At the end of each lesson, questions taken directly from that lesson's material provide a chance for your kids to show what they have learned (most kids find this to be *a lot* of fun).

The lessons in this book, although kid-friendly, are not fluff. They contain solid theological truth about Christ that will be like good seed planted in their hearts. Recently, I heard the moving testimony of a man who had gone through a series of trials so devastating that he almost walked away from his faith. After coming through his crisis, he said, "It wasn't what I didn't know about Jesus that brought me back—it was what I *did* know." When I heard that, I knew the hard work of writing a book like this was not in vain. My hope is that the truths found in this book may one day keep others anchored to Christ in the midst of their own trials.

Now get the kids, a cup of coffee, and let's begin our journey with Jesus.

HOW TO USE THIS BOOK

Here are a few tips on how to use *Teach Your Kids About Jesus* and what you can expect to gain from it.

READ THE BIBLE PASSAGE FIRST

First and foremost, let me emphasize that this book is designed to be used as a companion to the Bible, not as a substitute for it. Each lesson is based on a certain Bible passage, so you should read the passage first (the chapter and verse are given at the top of each lesson). Resist the temptation to read the lesson on its own without having first read the Scripture passage. They are designed to work together.

AS PART OF YOUR HOMESCHOOL CURRICULUM

Many homeschool parents want to incorporate the Bible somehow into their child's curriculum. *Teach Your Kids About Jesus* fits that need perfectly due to its simple format and the short amount of time required for each lesson.

AS A SUPER KID-FRIENDLY FAMILY DEVOTIONAL

As I was preparing the lessons for this book, our family would spend about fifteen minutes each morning going through them and the kids really had a blast. Each one loved to read the Scripture (though our four-year-old needed a little help) and then the lesson as well. I would read it last, and then they would take turns answering the questions which to them was great fun!

AS A WAY TO INTRODUCE YOUR CHILD TO JESUS

Many parents want to introduce their children to Jesus and the Bible, but they feel intimidated by the size and seeming difficulty of the Bible itself. Because of its singular focus, *Teach Your Kids About Jesus* is a great starting point for getting to know the person of Jesus and the high points of the Gospels.

YOU SET THE STYLE AND PACE

Each of the lessons can be as short or long as you want to make them. Some lessons may spark more questions than others. Also, take advantage of those moments when your child shows special interest in a certain lesson. One of our children especially loved the multiple choice questions and insisted on answering them—and that was fine with me. You might even try offering some chocolate chips as an incentive for getting the right answers!

READ THE LESSON MORE THAN ONCE

You can do these lessons anytime you choose, but whenever you do them, I suggest you read each lesson twice or perhaps even three times. This will help you and your kids understand and retain the material. Repetition is the mother of learning.

READ WITH ENTHUSIASM AND EXPRESSION

Reading with a monotone will surely put your listeners to sleep no matter how astute they are. Your kids will be drawn into the lessons when you read with lots of expression. They will catch on to your enthusiasm for the material and reflect that in their own reading as well.

A NOTE CONCERNING VOCABULARY AND FIGURATIVE LANGUAGE

I have purposely tried to communicate theological concepts such as redemption, repentance, propitiation, and atonement in clear and simple terms without losing the meaning of the words themselves. Likewise, because children tend to be very literal in their thinking, I have (as a general rule) sought to express figurative language in more literal or concrete terms. For example, the word "heart" is often explained in terms of thoughts, feelings, and understanding.

A NOTE ABOUT THE QUESTIONS FOR EACH LESSON

As you go through the book, you will often find a question that is repeated from another lesson. If the answer is not in the previous lesson, there will be a reference to the lesson where the answer can be found. There is also an answer key in the back of the book.

BY THE TIME YOU'RE DONE

By the time you have finished this book, you and your family will know a lot about who Jesus is, what he was like, what he taught, and what he accomplished. You will have a better understanding of the Bible—especially the Gospels. And hopefully, you will have a deeper desire to know more about all that Jesus said and did.

CONCERNING PRONOUNS THAT REFER TO CHRIST

Due to the number of pronouns that refer to Jesus (such as "he" and "his"), I have chosen not to capitalize each one. As you can tell from the overall tone of the book, this is not meant as a lack of respect for Christ. It is simply a choice I have made for ease of reading and to minimize distractions from the text.

EXTRAS ONLINE

The website that accompanies this book (www.TeachYourKidsAboutJesus.com) has many extra resources to aid you in your study of the life of Jesus. Bookmark it and visit often!

PART I

FROM BIRTH TO THE BATTLE IN THE WILDERNESS

LESSON ONE

WHERE DID JESUS COME FROM?

1 JOHN 4:9

God sent His one and only Son into the world. This is what the Bible tells us. Jesus was sent from Heaven by God.

But what did that look like? Did he come on a spaceship? Did he come down on a ladder or a rope? Well, not quite. In our next lesson, we will see just how Jesus came into the world.

QUESTIONS:

1. Who sent Jesus into the world?
2. Jesus was God's one and only _Son_ .
3. We learn about Jesus by reading the _bible_ .

Answers on page 159.

LESSON TWO

A CHILD IS BORN

MATTHEW 1:18-25

Long ago, God gave this promise to a man named Isaiah: "A virgin will be with child and will give birth to a son, and they will call him Immanuel" (Matthew 1:23).

This is how Jesus came. No spaceships. No ladders or ropes. It was even more amazing than that. A young girl named Mary was told by an angel that she, by the power of the Holy Spirit and without a human father, was going to have a very special baby. Nine months later, Jesus was born. God's promise to Isaiah had finally been fulfilled.

The birth of Jesus was a miracle—something that only God could make happen. His birth still amazes us, and as we will find out from a closer look at his name, Jesus' birth is not the only thing that was amazing.

QUESTIONS:

1. How did Jesus come into the world?
    (a) on a spaceship
    (b) by magic
    (c) as a baby boy

2. True or false: Jesus' birth was something that only God could make happen.

3. A young girl named ____Mary____ gave birth to Jesus.

4. True or false: Mary was told by an angel that she, by the power of the Holy Spirit, without a human father, was going to have a very special baby.

Answers on page 159.

4

LESSON THREE

IMMANUEL

MATTHEW 1:18-23

Names often have special meanings. Jesus has another name, *Immanuel*, and it certainly means something special. *Immanuel* means "God with us."

When Jesus was sent by God, he came as a special baby with a special name. The person Isaiah spoke about was not just a person like us. He was God as well! Jesus was *Immanuel*—God with us.

QUESTIONS:

1. *Immanuel* means ___God with us___.
2. What is one thing about Jesus that makes him very different from us?
3. *True* or false: Though Jesus was a real person born into the world, he was also God.
4. How did Jesus come into the world?

    (a) on a spaceship

    (b) by magic

    (c) as a baby boy

Answers on page 159.

LESSON FOUR

WHY JESUS CAME

MATTHEW 1:21-23

Immanuel is actually a second name for Jesus. It tells us who he is. His first name, on the other hand, tells us more about why he was sent into the world. The name *Jesus* comes from the Hebrew name for God, and it means "the LORD saves." In the Bible, to save means to rescue someone or set someone free from trouble. Jesus was sent into the world on a rescue mission. He was sent to save someone from terrible trouble. He was sent to set someone free.

QUESTIONS:

1. *Immanuel* means _God with us_ .
2. *Jesus* means _the lord saves_ .
3. Though Jesus was a real person born into the world, he was also _God_ .
4. Why was Jesus sent into the world?
    (a) to make it a nicer place to live
    (b) on a rescue mission
    (c) to set a good example

Answers on page 159.

LESSON FIVE

SLAVES

MATTHEW 1:21; JOHN 8:34-36

In the Old Testament, God's people had been slaves in Egypt. When Jesus came, they were no longer in Egypt, but they were still slaves who needed to be rescued and set free.

Before Jesus was born, his parents were told, "He will save his people from their sins" (Matthew 1:21). Later, Jesus said, "Everyone who practices sin is a *slave to sin*," and "if the Son [Jesus] sets you free, you will be really free" (John 8:34-36). But what does that mean? And what does it mean to be a "slave to sin?"

In Scripture, a "slave to sin" is someone who gives himself to pride, disobedience, and selfishness—what Jesus calls *sin*. This is someone whose thoughts, desires, and feelings are not free to love and serve the God who created him. This kind of person is willingly ruled by an attitude of pride that says, "I have no need for God," and so he seeks to live without Him. He thinks that life apart from God is freedom, but it is actually slavery because he is held captive by his own pride and rebellious attitudes. The bad news is that we all come into the world this way, but the good news is that God has done something about it.

So, God's people were no longer slaves to men, but slaves to sin—and Jesus had come to set them free.

QUESTIONS:

1. In what country had God's people been slaves?

2. Jesus was on a _____ mission.

3. Why was Jesus sent to rescue God's people?

4. A person who is held captive by his own pride and rebellious attitudes is

    (a) cool

    (b) wise

    (c) a slave to sin

5. Which name given to Jesus means "the LORD saves?"

Answers on page 160.

LESSON SIX

WHERE JESUS LIVED

LUKE 2:4-7, 39-40

Jesus was born in a very small town called *Bethlehem*, which means "house of bread," but he spent most of his life in Nazareth. Bethlehem was in the southern part of Israel in the region of Judea. Nazareth, on the other hand, was in the northern part of Israel, in the region of Galilee. Neither town was thought of as being very important at all.

Now this is not where you might expect the Son of God to be born. In fact, Matthew 21:5 says of Jesus, "Look, your king is coming to you." Since he was a king, shouldn't he have been born into a royal family that lived in a king's palace? Maybe. But one can hardly learn to be a servant in a royal family, and as Jesus would say later on, "the Son of Man did not come to be served, but to serve" (Mark 10:45).

QUESTIONS:

1. Where was Jesus born?

2. Where did he live most of his life?

    (a) Nazareth

    (b) Bethlehem

    (c) South Carolina

3. Why do you think his heavenly Father did not send him to a family of great royalty?

4. Jesus was sent to save his people from their _____ .

5. What does the name *Bethlehem* mean?

Answers on page 160.

LESSON SEVEN

GROWING UP

LUKE 2:39-40

Growing up in Nazareth, Jesus would have played, eaten, and done many of the things little boys love to do. Joseph, his earthly father, was a carpenter and he would have taught Jesus how to work with wood.

School was also a big part of his life. Like us, he learned to read, write, and count. As a Jewish boy, Jesus also spent lots of time reading and memorizing the Hebrew Scriptures (what we call the Old Testament), and that seems to be what he loved most.

QUESTIONS:

1. What things did Jesus learn in school?
2. What part of the Bible did Jesus study and memorize?
3. Jesus grew up in _____ .
4. Who was Joseph and what kind of work did he do?

Answers on page 160.

LESSON EIGHT

AT THE TEMPLE

LUKE 2:39-52

As Jesus learned the Scriptures, we are told he was "filled with wisdom" and that he "increased in wisdom"(Luke 2:40, 52). When he was twelve, he made his way to the Temple in Jerusalem where the people came to worship God. The gospel of Luke tells us that while he was there, he was sitting with the teachers listening to them and asking them questions. As the teachers listened, they were amazed at his understanding and answers.

His parents were worried about him because they did not know where he was. When they finally found him, he said to them, "Did you not know that I must be in my Father's house and about my Father's business?"

Jesus' words show us that even at a young age he knew that he was on a special mission from his heavenly Father. It was just a matter of time.

QUESTIONS:

1. As Jesus studied the Scriptures, he was filled with _wisdom_ and he _increased_ in wisdom.

2. Where did the people in Jerusalem go to worship God?

3. What was Jesus doing in the Temple when he was twelve?

    (a) hiding from his parents

    (b) playing with his friends

    (c) listening to the teachers and asking them questions

4. Did Jesus know that God had a special purpose for his life?

Answers on page 160.

LESSON NINE

PREPARING THE WAY

MARK 1:1-8

God chose a man named John the Baptist to announce that the King promised in the Old Testament was about to come. John told the people to get ready for the King by turning away from their sins. Those who listened and believed him were baptized in the Jordan River.

You might ask, "What is baptism?" Well, baptism can be described in many ways, but let's try to be as simple as we can. Baptism is being placed under water and then lifted out of the water as a sign that something special has happened to us—that we have had a change of mind about ourselves and about God. Instead of loving to be selfish and disobedient, we now have turned to God for forgiveness of our selfish and sinful ways and have given ourselves to Him. Being baptized is also a way of saying to others, "I now belong to Jesus."

By preaching and baptizing, John prepared the people for the ministry of Jesus. As we will see, however, not everyone liked John and the message God had given him.

QUESTIONS:

1. True or false: Baptism is a sign that we have turned to God for forgiveness of our selfish and sinful ways and have given ourselves to Him.
2. Whom did God choose to prepare the people for the coming King?
3. Who was the King that John spoke about?
4. True or false: Baptism is a way of saying to others, "I now belong to Jesus."

Answers on page 160.

LESSON TEN

THE KING HAS ENEMIES

MATTHEW 3:1-10

As John the Baptist preached about Jesus, God's coming King, we read of a very important group of people called the *Pharisees*.

The word *Pharisee* means "separated one." These were the religious teachers in Israel who told the people what God expected of them. They were very strict about keeping all of God's laws, and they even made up rules for people to keep that God had not given. However, God was not pleased with them because they had become proud, self-righteous, unkind, and unmerciful.

Worst of all, the Pharisees would stop at nothing to keep Jesus from carrying out his rescue mission because he made it clear that they too were blinded by their sin.

QUESTIONS:

1. The _Pharisee_ taught the people about God.
2. The Pharisees were very strict about keeping God's _law_ .
3. True or false: The Pharisees were known for being kind and merciful.
4. Why did the Pharisees not see who Jesus really was?
5. Who was God's coming King?
   Jesus

Answers on page 161.

LESSON ELEVEN

JESUS IS BAPTIZED

MATTHEW 3:13-17

Learning to wait is one of the hardest things we will ever have to do. Jesus knew well what it was like to wait. He had to wait for the right time to carry out his mission from the Father. He waited until he was thirty years old to begin his public ministry. It began with his own baptism by John the Baptist.

The gospel of Matthew says, "After Jesus was baptized, just as he was coming up out of the water, the heavens opened and he saw the Spirit of God descending like a dove and coming on him. And a voice from heaven said, 'This is my one dear Son; in him I take great delight' " (Matthew 3:16-17).

Try to imagine the scene—Heaven opening, the Spirit coming down, and the voice of the Father being heard. And beyond that, we need to ask a very important question: why would Jesus need to be baptized at all? We will try to answer that question in our next lesson.

QUESTIONS:

1. How old was Jesus when he was baptized? 30
2. Whose voice came from Heaven when Jesus was baptized? god the father
3. What did the voice say?
4. True or false: Baptism is a sign that we have turned to God for forgiveness of our selfish and sinful ways and have given ourselves to Him (lesson 9).
5. True or false: Jesus was sent to set God's people free from sin (lesson 5).

Answers on page 161.

LESSON TWELVE

FOR US

EPHESIANS 5:2

Scripture teaches that Jesus "loved us and gave himself for us" (Ephesians 5:2). Those two little words "for us" may be the most important words in the entire Bible. They tell us why God the Father sent His Son into the world. They describe everything Jesus did in his earthly life, including his baptism.

Baptism is a sign that our sins have been forgiven, but Jesus had no sin that needed to be forgiven. He never disobeyed his Father's commands. Jesus came into the world to take away *our* sin—to rescue *us* from slavery to sin.

The baptism of Jesus pointed to the day that he would die for us and be buried in a borrowed tomb. But not only that. Just as he rose from the waters of the Jordan, he would also rise from the dead and never die again.

QUESTIONS:

1. Christ loved us and gave himself _____ .

2. What two words may be the most important words in the entire Bible?

    (a) for us

    (b) Jesus wept

    (c) ignorant brothers

3. True or false: Jesus never sinned.

4. True or false: Baptism is a sign that we have turned to God for forgiveness of our selfish and sinful ways and have given ourselves to Him.

5. Jesus' baptism pointed to the day that he would _____ for us, be buried, and rise again from the dead.

Answers on page 161.

LESSON 13

THE FATHER LOVES THE SON

MARK 1:9-11

The task that God gave to His Son would not be easy. Jesus knew that he would have many disappointments and that he would be a "man of sorrows." Eventually, it would seem as if the whole world was against him. He would even feel as if the Father had forsaken him.

But as the heavens opened at his baptism, the Father declared His great love for Jesus. "You are my one dear Son; in you I take great delight" (Mark 1:11). This was not the last time Jesus would hear these words. Later on, Jesus would even say, "As the Father has loved me, I have also loved you" (John 15:9).

Throughout his ministry, Jesus was certain of his Father's love, and therefore he never gave up on the work he was sent to do.

QUESTIONS:

1. What did the Father say at Jesus' baptism?
2. Jesus was certain of his Father's _____ .
3. Because of his Father's love for him, Jesus never _____ .
4. True or false: Christ loved us and gave his life for us.

Answers on page 161.

LESSON 14

THE HOLY SPIRIT COMES UPON JESUS

MARK 1:9-11

In lesson 3 we learned that Jesus was fully God (Immanuel). But he was also fully man. As a man, Jesus would be strengthened by the Spirit of God. Acts 10:38 says, "God anointed him with the Holy Spirit and with power. He went around doing good and healing all who were oppressed by the devil, because God was with him."

At his baptism, Jesus was given power for his ministry by the Holy Spirit who came down on him "like a dove" (Mark 1:10). The Holy Spirit of God was with him and in him, filling him with power and grace. He was Jesus' constant companion.

QUESTIONS:

1. Jesus saw Heaven open and the _____ coming down on him like a dove.
2. True or false: God anointed Jesus of Nazareth with the Holy Spirit and power.
3. Jesus was given power for his _____ .
4. The Holy Spirit was with Jesus and _____ him.

Answers on page 162.

LESSON 15

JESUS IN THE WILDERNESS

MATTHEW 4:1-11

Some tests show what we know, but other tests show what we are. Jesus was put to the test by the temptations of the devil. How he responded to those temptations would show who he really was.

Would he be obedient to the Father? Would he trust the Father? Or would he give in to the devil's trickery and fail the test?

If he failed, the mission would be over.

QUESTIONS:

1. Who tempted Jesus in the wilderness?
2. True or false: Jesus' obedience and trust in his Father would be put to the test.
3. True or false: Jesus would have to face his temptations alone without the Holy Spirit.
4. The Holy Spirit was _____ Jesus and _____ him (lesson 14).

Answers on page 162.

LESSON 16

JESUS, FULL OF THE SPIRIT

LUKE 3:21-22; LUKE 4:1-2

Jesus was in the wilderness for forty days with nothing to eat. During that time he was tempted by the devil. His body grew weaker with each passing day, and he desperately needed food.

How could he stand against so great an enemy when he himself was so weak?

The gospel of Luke gives us the answer: "Jesus, full of the Holy Spirit... was led by the Spirit" (4:1). Jesus was not alone. At his baptism, the Holy Spirit came on him like a dove, and he was still with him and in him.

Jesus would pass this test in the power of the Holy Spirit.

QUESTIONS:

1. What did Jesus eat in the wilderness?
2. How long was he in the wilderness?
3. Would Jesus have to face his temptations alone?
4. The gospel of Luke says Jesus was _____ of the Holy Spirit.

Answers on page 162.

LESSON 17

HAND-TO-HAND COMBAT

MATTHEW 4:4, 7, 10; EPHESIANS 6:10-17

Roman soldiers often used a short, dagger-like weapon for hand-to-hand combat. Ephesians 6:17 compares the Scriptures to that weapon by calling Scripture the "sword of the Spirit." Jesus needed such a weapon because he was in a fierce battle. The truth of the Bible would be his "sword" as he fought the lies and tricks of the devil.

The devil wanted to stop Jesus from carrying out God's plan of saving His people, so he came against Jesus with all his might.

How would Jesus defeat the devil? By using the sword of the Spirit—the very words of God he had been learning and memorizing since he was a little boy.

QUESTIONS:

1. How would Jesus defeat the devil?
   (a) by his own power
   (b) by having a positive attitude
   (c) by using the sword of the Spirit
2. True or false: The devil wanted to stop Jesus from doing his Father's will.
3. What is the "sword of the Spirit"?
4. True or false: Jesus had to face his temptations alone.

Answers on page 162.

LESSON 18

SAME OLD TRICKS

GENESIS 3:1-6; HEBREWS 4:14-15

In the Garden of Eden, the devil tricked Eve into believing him and not trusting God. He tried the same thing with Jesus. If Jesus had believed the devil and had not trusted and obeyed God, the devil would have won the battle. But Jesus was ready—he had the sword.

Jesus grew up learning the Scriptures and he knew them well. As we will see, each time he was tempted, he would respond with Scripture. In fact, he used three verses from the Old Testament book called Deuteronomy to defeat his deadly foe. We will learn more about this in our next few lessons.

QUESTIONS:

1. The devil tricked Eve into not trusting _____ .
2. How would Jesus be able to defeat the devil?
3. Jesus used _____ verses from the book of _____ .
4. True or false: Jesus was not quite ready for the devil's trickery.

Answers on page 162.

LESSON 19

A TEST OF OBEDIENCE

MATTHEW 4:1-4; DEUTERONOMY 8:3

Jesus had been in the wilderness for forty days without food. He was starving and the devil knew it. Satan said to Jesus, "If you are the Son of God, command these stones to become bread" (Matthew 4:3). Where is the temptation here? Surely it would not be a sin to eat after being without food for so long.

The devil was tempting Jesus to act apart from his Father's will. But for Jesus, obedience to God was more important than satisfying his own hunger. So he answered, "It is written: 'Man does not live by bread alone, but by every word that comes from the mouth of God' " (4:4).

He would later say, "My food is to do the will of the one who sent me and to complete his work" (John 4:34). The most important thing for Jesus was to live a life of complete and total obedience to God the Father.

QUESTIONS:

1. How long did Jesus go without food?
2. Jesus was being tempted to act apart from his Father's _____ .
3. True or false: Jesus said, "My food is to do the will of the one who sent me and to complete his work."
4. True or false: Man lives by bread alone.

Answers on page 163.

LESSON 20

A TEST OF TRUST

MATTHEW 4:5-7; DEUTERONOMY 6:16

From high up on the Temple, the devil said to Jesus, "Throw yourself down" (Matthew 4:5). He then misused a verse from Psalm 91 that speaks of God's promise to take care of His people. Much like he did with Eve in the Garden of Eden, the devil tried to make Jesus doubt what God had said: "Do you really trust God?" Or better yet, "Can God really be trusted? Throw yourself down and let's find out."

Jesus answered, "It is also written: 'You are not to put the Lord your God to the test' " (4:7). He made it clear to the devil that he trusted God, but he would not disobey God in order to prove that trust.

Jesus showed his trust by his obedience, and he defeated another temptation.

QUESTIONS:

1. How did Jesus show his trust in God?
2. True or false: The devil misused a verse from Psalm 91 to tempt Jesus.
3. Whose will did Jesus obey?
4. What is the "sword of the Spirit"?
5. Jesus defeated the devil with three verses from
   (a) the book of Genesis
   (b) the book of Deuteronomy
   (c) the book of Noah

Answers on page 163.

LESSON 21

A TEST OF WORSHIP

MATTHEW 4:6-11; DEUTERONOMY 6:13

Jesus once asked, "What good will it be for a man if he gains the whole world yet loses his soul?" The answer to his question is clear: it would not be good at all. Yet that is what the devil promised to give Jesus—all the kingdoms of the world and their splendor—if Jesus would only bow down and worship him.

This was a final, desperate attempt to ruin Jesus' mission by tricking him into disobeying God. But as he had done before, Jesus trusted in the Scriptures and replied, "Go away, Satan! For it is written: 'You are to worship the Lord your God and serve only him' " (Matthew 4:10).

For Jesus, obedience and faithfulness to God were worth far more than all the kingdoms of the world. This battle was over, and the devil went on his way—at least for a while.

QUESTIONS:

1. What did the devil want from Jesus?
2. The devil offered Jesus all the _____ .
3. True or false: Jesus gave in to the devil's temptations.
4. Jesus used three verses from the book of _____ to defeat the devil.
5. For Jesus, what two things are worth more than having all the kingdoms of the world?

Answers on page 163.

PART II

WHAT KIND OF PERSON WAS JESUS?

LESSON 22

JESUS, FULL OF GRACE AND TRUTH

JOHN 1:1-5, 14

The gospel of John says of Jesus, "We have seen his glory, the glory of the One and Only who came from the Father, full of grace and truth" (John 1:14, NIV).

Jesus was unlike any man John had ever known. As one of his disciples, John walked with Jesus day and night for three years. He watched his every move. He listened to his every word. John seemed to be amazed that Jesus would love him. He even referred to himself as "the disciple whom Jesus loved." As he sat down to write about Jesus, his amazement made its way into these words: *full of grace and truth*.

QUESTIONS:

1. How does the Apostle John describe Jesus?

2. How many years did John walk with Jesus?

3. The Apostle John wrote the _____ of John.

4. True or false: John was amazed that Jesus would love him.

5. Who was with and in Jesus as his constant companion (lesson 14)?

Answers on page 163.

LESSON 23

JESUS TOUCHES PEOPLE WITH GRACE

MARK 1:40-45

In lesson 22 we learned that Jesus was "full of grace." What does that mean and what does it look like? It means that Jesus loves the unlovable. His grace even goes so far as to touch the untouchable—like those with a terrible skin disease called *leprosy*.

The Pharisees—those men who taught the people about God—would never touch anyone with leprosy for fear of making themselves "unclean." But Jesus would.

Once, a man with leprosy begged Jesus to heal him and make him clean saying, "If you are willing you can make me clean." The gospel of Mark tells us Jesus' response. "Moved with compassion, Jesus stretched out his hand and touched him, saying, 'I am willing. Be clean!' The leprosy left him at once, and he was clean" (Mark 1:41-42).

Jesus did this many times with many people. He touched those no one else would touch because he was full of grace. This too was part of his rescue mission.

QUESTIONS:

1. Jesus loves the unlovable and touches the _____ .
2. Were the Pharisees willing to touch people with leprosy?
3. True or false: Jesus was moved with compassion as he touched the sick man.
4. What does the name *Jesus* mean (lesson 4)?
5. What does the name *Immanuel* mean (lesson 3)?

Answers on page 164.

LESSON 24

EATING WITH TAX COLLECTORS AND SINNERS

MARK 2:13-17

Tax collectors and sinners were some of the "unlovables" in Jesus' day. Tax collectors would often take more money from people than they should have, and the group known as "sinners" were frowned upon by the Pharisees because of their openly sinful ways of living. These people had no friends and no one willing to love them. No one, that is, until Jesus came.

Jesus was known for spending time with them in the countryside and in their homes, often sharing a meal together. Mark tells us, "As Jesus was having a meal in Levi's home, many tax collectors and sinners were eating with Jesus and his disciples, for there were many who followed him. When the experts in the law and the Pharisees saw that he was eating with sinners and tax collectors, they said to his disciples, "Why does he eat with tax collectors and sinners?" When Jesus heard this he said to them, "Those who are healthy don't need a physician, but those who are sick do. I have not come to call the righteous, but sinners" (Mark 2:15-17).

This is the grace of Jesus. He comes to the lowest of the low—to those whom no one else cares about. And though he is both God and King, he is not embarrassed to eat with tax collectors and sinners.

QUESTIONS:

1. True or false: Tax collectors and sinners were "unlovables."
2. True or false: The Pharisees were willing to eat with tax collectors and sinners.
3. What did Jesus say to the Pharisees?
4. Jesus is not _____ to eat with tax collectors and sinners.
5. Jesus was full of _____ and _____ .

Answers on page 164.

LESSON 25

SURPRISED BY THE GRACE OF JESUS

LUKE 8:40-48

Jesus was busy with ministry and surrounded by a large crowd of people. Suddenly, a desperate woman pressed her way through the crowd and reached for the edge of his garment. She had been sick for twelve years, but as soon as she touched Jesus, she was healed. Now for a woman to touch a teacher like this in public was unheard of, nor would anyone have wanted to touch her for fear of being made unclean (unfit to worship God).

But Jesus stopped, turned around and said, "Who touched me?" The woman, filled with fear, fell down at his feet and told him everything. Much to her surprise, Jesus did not scold her for touching him or getting in his way. Rather, he spoke these gentle words to her: "Daughter, your faith has made you well. Go in peace" (Luke 8:48).

The woman went away healed, amazed, and loved. She had just met the Lord Jesus, the man of the Spirit, full of grace and truth.

QUESTIONS:

1. What did Jesus say to the woman who touched him?
2. How did Jesus respond to the woman's request?
   (a) He laughed at her
   (b) He got angry
   (c) He spoke gently to her and healed her disease
3. True or false: The woman went away fearful.
4. Who was with and in Jesus as his constant companion (lesson 14)?

Answers on page 164.

LESSON 26

JESUS, A MAN OF TRUTH

JOHN 18:36-38

Jesus came into a world that was very confused about God. He talked with many different people who had many different ideas about what God was like. How can we know God? How should we worship Him?

Part of Jesus' mission was to bring the truth about the Father. He came to show the world how to know and worship Him. That is why he said, "For this reason I came into the world—to testify to the truth" (John 18:37).

QUESTIONS:

1. True or false: The world was very confused about God.

2. Jesus came to bring the _____ about the _____ .

3. Jesus was "full of grace and _____ ."

4. Jesus came to show the world how to

   (a) be like the Pharisees

   (b) be nice to one another

   (c) know and worship God

Answers on page 164.

31

LESSON 27

LISTEN TO HIM

MARK 9:2-7

As before with the crowds, once again the Father's voice came from Heaven saying to Peter, James, and John, "This is my one dear Son. Listen to him!" (Mark 9:7).

Why would the Father say, "Listen to him?" Because Jesus came to tell them the truth they needed to hear. Many times as Jesus taught, he would begin by saying, "Truly, truly I say to you." He was telling them what the Father had told them: "Listen! Pay attention! If you really want to know God, then give me your ears."

So Jesus says, "Truly, truly, I say to you," and the Father says, "This is my one dear Son. Listen to him!"

QUESTIONS:

1. What did Jesus often say as he taught the people?
2. What did the Father say about Jesus?
3. What did Jesus show us how to do?
   (a) know and worship God
   (b) ignore God
   (c) be like the Pharisees
4. True or false: The world was confused about God.

Answers on page 164.

LESSON 28

THE WAY, THE TRUTH, AND THE LIFE

JOHN 14:6

Jesus came to a world that was lost and confused. They had lost sight of truth and were confused about the will of God. In Old Testament language, they were living in "darkness." But Jesus came as a light in that darkness to show the way back to the Father.

He said to his disciples, "I am the way, and the truth, and the life. No one comes to the Father except through me" (John 14:6).

Here is what we need to know: Jesus is the truth! He is the truth about God, and he is the only way to the Father.

QUESTIONS:

1. Jesus said, "I am the _____ and the _____ and the _____ ."

2. According to Jesus, how many ways are there to the Father?

   (a) as many as we want

   (b) only one

   (c) 50

3. True or false: The Father said, "This is my one dear Son. Listen to him!"

4. What did Jesus often say as he taught the people?

5. True or false: Jesus taught the people they could believe whatever they wanted to about God.

Answers on page 165.

LESSON 29

JESUS LOVED PEOPLE

EPHESIANS 3:14-19

What a person is like is often determined by what he loves. The Gospels tell us that the Pharisees and teachers of the Law loved to be seen praying. They loved the most important seats in the synagogues and to be greeted in public. They loved money and they loved praise from men more than praise from God.

They were not like Jesus, and the people knew it.

While the Pharisees loved power and popularity, Jesus loved people. He loved tax collectors and sinners. He loved Martha and her sister Mary. He loved Lazarus. He loved his disciples. He even loved the Pharisees and prayed for their forgiveness.

Jesus loved people. He loved sinful people. He loved them then and he loves them now.

QUESTIONS:

1. The Pharisees loved praise from men more than _____ .
2. True or false: The Pharisees were a lot like Jesus.
3. Jesus loves _____ .
4. What kinds of people does Jesus love?
    (a) only good people
    (b) sinful people
    (c) only people who go to church
5. Give the names of two people Jesus loved.

Answers on page 165.

PART III

THE MINISTRY OF JESUS

LESSON 30

JESUS' MINISTRY BEGINS

LUKE 3:23; 4:14; ACTS 10:38

After Jesus was baptized by John and tempted for forty days by the devil, he began his ministry. According to Luke's gospel, he was about thirty years old. For the next three years, Jesus traveled around Israel in the Spirit's power—teaching, healing the sick, doing miracles, and calling people to follow him. Through him the world would come to know God's truth, God's will, and God's grace as it had never known before.

Jesus would willingly fulfill his mission as one who "did not come to be served but to serve, and to give his life as a ransom for many" (Mark 10:45). But as we briefly mentioned in lesson 10, he would have plenty of trouble along the way.

QUESTIONS:

1. How old was Jesus when he began his ministry?
2. How long would his ministry (traveling around Israel) last?
3. True or false: God anointed Jesus with the Holy Spirit and power.
4. During Jesus' ministry, he would teach people, heal the sick, do miracles, and call people to _____ .
5. True or false: Jesus came to be served by people.

Answers on page 165.

LESSON 31

JESUS PREACHES IN HIS HOMETOWN

LUKE 4:14-30

The news about Jesus quickly spread throughout the countryside of Galilee. He taught in the synagogues and everyone praised him. Then Jesus went to his hometown of Nazareth. One day in the synagogue, he began to read an Old Testament passage (Isaiah 61) that spoke of the life and ministry of the Messiah, God's anointed Savior.

This is what Jesus read:

> The Spirit of the Lord is upon me,
> because he has anointed me
> to proclaim good news to the poor.
> He has sent me to proclaim release to the captives
> and the regaining of sight to the blind,
> to set free those who are oppressed,
> to proclaim the year of the Lord's favor.

After Jesus read this, he said, "Today this Scripture has been fulfilled even as you heard it being read" (Luke 4:21). Jesus said that *he* was the great Messiah they had been waiting for.

The people were amazed at his gracious words and they all spoke well of him. But within a few moments, that would quickly change.

QUESTIONS:

1. What Old Testament passage did Jesus read from?
2. True or false: The Messiah is God's Anointed Savior.
3. Jesus said, "Today this Scripture has been _____ ."
4. According to Jesus, who was the Messiah the people had been waiting for?
5. True or false: All the people in the synagogue were angry when Jesus read from Isaiah.

Answers on page 165.

LESSON 32

THE TRUTH CAUSED TROUBLE IN NAZARETH

LUKE 4:14-30

Remember that Jesus was full of grace and truth. He tells us the truth about God and about ourselves so we can know and do God's will.

The Old Testament records how the Jewish people often rebelled against God and the prophets He sent to them. To their surprise, Jesus begins to remind his hometown listeners of this folly. He tells them that they will rebel against God the same way, and as a result God would pour out His blessings on the *Gentiles* (those who are not Jewish).

All the people were furious when they heard this. Can you imagine? One moment they all spoke well of Jesus, and the next, they were chasing him out of Nazareth and trying to throw him off of a cliff!

When proud people are rebuked, the response is usually anger. Jesus' words greatly offended these people and so they tried to kill him. As the apostle John said, "He came to what was his own, but his own people did not receive him" (John 1:11).

QUESTIONS:

1. Does Jesus tell us the truth about God only?

2. True or false: God's people Israel, the Jews, have always been obedient to Him.

3. Did Jesus tell his hometown listeners what they wanted to hear?

4. Jesus is full of grace and _____ .

5. What Old Testament book was Jesus reading from that day in the synagogue?

    (a) Genesis

    (b) Isaiah

    (c) Jonah

6. What is a *Gentile*?

Answers on page 166.

LESSON 33

DOWN TO CAPERNAUM

MATTHEW 4:12-17

Unwelcome in his hometown, Jesus went to live in Capernaum, a city close to the Sea of Galilee. *Capernaum* means "village of Nahum." It was far away from Jerusalem and had a large number of Gentiles living there. Jesus ministered in and around Capernaum for most of his three year public ministry.

Jesus would later predict judgment against the city for not being willing to repent, even though they had seen him work many miracles.

QUESTIONS:

1. Where did Jesus choose to live after he was chased out of Nazareth?
    (a) Capernaum
    (b) Jerusalem
    (c) New York
2. What does *Capernaum* mean?
3. True or false: Many Gentiles lived in Capernaum.
4. Back in Nazareth, the people tried to throw Jesus off of a _____ .
5. What is a Gentile?

Answers on page 166.

LESSON 34

THE MESSIAH'S MESSAGE

MATTHEW 4:12-17

After John the Baptist was put in prison, Jesus went into Galilee and proclaimed the good news of God. "The time is fulfilled," he said, "and the Kingdom of God is near. Repent and believe the gospel!" (Mark 1:15). As we will see later, Jesus taught many great things, but the Gospel writers sum up his message in this sentence, "Repent, for the Kingdom of Heaven is near."

This was the good news of God: "The Kingdom of God is near!" As we saw in lesson 31, it was the good news the Messiah came to bring. The great King had come and it was time to establish his Kingdom.

We will take a closer look at this again in some later lessons, but for now, just remember that the Kingdom of God was the main message of Jesus' ministry everywhere he went.

QUESTIONS:

1. After John the Baptist was put in prison, where did Jesus go? And what did he do?
2. Jesus said, "Repent, for the _____ is near."
3. True or false: Jesus never told anyone to repent or turn from their sins.
4. What was the main message of Jesus' ministry?
5. True or false: The Messiah is God's anointed Savior.

Answers on page 166.

LESSON 35

JESUS CHOOSES HIS DISCIPLES

MARK 1:16-20; MARK 3:13-19

"Follow me," Jesus said to Simon and Andrew as they were fishing in the sea of Galilee. "I will turn you into fishers of people" (Mark 1:17). At once, the brothers left their nets and followed Jesus. A few moments later, the same thing happened to two other brothers, James and John. They were also fishermen.

These were the first disciples that Jesus called to follow him. He would soon choose eight more, and these men would eventually become known as the Twelve Apostles.

The word *apostle* means "one who is sent." For the next three years, Jesus would train them and then send them out to preach the message of the Kingdom.

QUESTIONS:

1. Jesus promised to make his disciples fishers of _____ .
2. Name two of Jesus' first disciples.
3. How many disciples did Jesus choose?
4. The disciples would become known as the Twelve _____ .
5. What message would the disciples preach?

Answers on page 166.

LESSON 36

WHAT IS A DISCIPLE?

MATTHEW 9:9; LUKE 6:40

In Jesus' time and even still today, a Jewish teacher called a *rabbi* would have students. These students were called *disciples*. The word *disciple* means "learner."

When Jesus chose his disciples, he often did so by saying, "Come, follow me." That is exactly what a disciple does: he follows his teacher everywhere, watches his every move, and listens to his every word. By careful and constant listening, the disciple memorized what the rabbi taught.

Jesus said this about being a disciple: "If anyone wants to serve me, he must follow me, and where I am, my servant will be too" (John 12:26), and "a disciple is not greater than his teacher, but everyone when fully trained will be like his teacher" (Luke 6:40). He would often say to people, "Take up your cross and follow me."

As Jesus says, the goal of the disciple is to become *like* his teacher. These days we use the term "Christian" much more than "disciple." But it is not possible to be a true Christian without being a disciple of Jesus. That is what this book is really all about— walking step by step with the Lord Jesus, learning about him, and seeking to become his disciple.

QUESTIONS:

1. A rabbi would have a group of students called _____ .

2. The word *disciple* means

    (a) musician

    (b) artist

    (c) learner

3. True or false: A disciple of Jesus seeks to be like Jesus by trying his best to be good.

4. Jesus often said, "Take up your cross and _____ ."

5. The goal of a disciple is to be _____ his teacher.

Answers on page 167.

LESSON 37

WHAT DID JESUS DO?

MATTHEW 4:23-25; MARK 6:30-34

During the early part of Jesus' ministry, he went throughout Galilee, teaching in their synagogues, preaching the good news of the Kingdom, and healing every disease and sickness among the people. As we will see in our next lesson, he also forgave sins.

All of the wonderful things Jesus said and did, especially his miracles of healing, caused large crowds to follow him everywhere. As he went from town to town the crowds grew bigger and bigger. And though he was often tired and weary, he always took time to care for them and love them.

QUESTIONS:

1. Which of the following did Jesus *not* do?
   (a) heal people
   (b) teach
   (c) preach about the Kingdom
   (d) waste time

2. What would especially cause large crowds to follow Jesus?

3. True or false: Although Jesus was often tired and weary, he always took time to care for people and love them.

4. Jesus often said, "Take up your cross and _____ ."

5. The goal of a disciple is to be _____ his teacher.

Answers on page 167.

LESSON 38

HEALING AND FORGIVING SINS

MATTHEW 9:1-8

Whenever we get sick or hurt, we often see a doctor so he can take care of our problem. Jesus is a kind of doctor as well, but he knows that we have a much bigger problem than being sick or hurt. And sometimes he takes care of that bigger problem first.

Here is a man who was brought to Jesus to have his legs healed, but instead, Jesus tells him, "Have courage, son! Your sins are forgiven" (Matthew 9:2).

Surely this is not what anyone expected to hear from Jesus, but as you read the Gospels, you find that Jesus does not always do what we might expect.

QUESTIONS:

1. Why did the man's friends bring him to Jesus?
2. Jesus said to the man, "Have courage, son! Your _____ are forgiven."
3. True or false: Jesus always does what we expect.
4. Jesus taught and preached the good news of the _____ .
5. Jesus promised to make his disciples:

   (a) better fishermen

   (b) rich

   (c) fishers of men

Answers on page 167.

45

LESSON 39

ANGRY AT JESUS

MATTHEW 9:1-8

The teachers of the Law knew that only God could forgive sins. So when they heard Jesus tell the paralyzed man that his sins were forgiven, they were furious. They understood that when Jesus said he had power to forgive sins, he was in fact claiming to be God. That is what made them so angry.

They were not willing to believe that Jesus was God's Son and that he had the same power and authority as the Father.

In our next lesson, we will see how Jesus uses this man's disability to show them that he really was Immanuel—God with us.

QUESTIONS:

1. Why were the teachers of the Law angry at Jesus?
2. The teachers of the Law knew that only _____ could forgive sins.
3. True or false: Because Jesus was God, he had the power and authority to forgive sins.
4. The teachers of the Law knew that Jesus was claiming to be _____ .
5. *Immanuel* means
   (a) Christ
   (b) teacher
   (c) God with us
   (d) rejoice

Answers on page 167.

LESSON 40

THE CROWDS WERE FILLED WITH AWE

MATTHEW 9:1-8

Which is easier: saying or doing? It is one thing to say "your sins are forgiven," but it is another thing altogether to tell a paralyzed man to "get up, take up your mat and go home." Jesus did both.

With one miraculous healing, Jesus proved to the unbelieving teachers of the law that he had authority on earth to forgive sins. Sadly, they remained in their unbelief.

At the same time, he did another thing that only God can do: he gave a crippled man the joy of walking by the very power of his words. Matthew ends this story by saying, "when the crowd saw this, they were filled with awe; and they praised God" (Matthew 9:8, NIV).

The Kingdom and power of God were right before their eyes. When we see Jesus in the Gospels, they are right before our eyes as well.

QUESTIONS:

1. What did Jesus say to the paralyzed man?

2. True or false: When the teachers of the law saw Jesus' power to heal, they praised God and worshiped him.

3. Jesus healed the crippled man by the power of his _____ .

4. When the crowds saw Jesus' power, they were

    (a) angry

    (b) confused

    (c) filled with awe

5. True or false: Because Jesus was God, he had the power and authority to forgive sins.

Answers on page 168.

LESSON 41

JESUS KNOWS OUR THOUGHTS

MATTHEW 9:1-4

When the Pharisees heard Jesus say, "Your sins are forgiven," they said he was blaspheming, or dishonoring God by claiming to do something that only God can do. At this point, we read, "Knowing their thoughts, Jesus said, 'Why do you entertain evil thoughts in your hearts?' " (Matthew 9:4, NIV).

Here is a glorious truth about Jesus that we do not want to miss: he knows our thoughts. He knows what is in our hearts and minds. "Why do you entertain evil thoughts *in your hearts*?" he asked them.

The Pharisees could not hide their thoughts from Jesus. Neither can we.

QUESTIONS:

1. The teachers of the Law knew that only _____ could forgive sins.
2. Jesus said "Why do you entertain evil thoughts in your _____ ."
3. What did Jesus tell the paralyzed man?
4. When Jesus said, "Your sins are forgiven," the teachers knew he was claiming to be _____ (lesson 39).
5. Jesus knows our _____ .
6. True or false: We can hide our thoughts from Jesus.

Answers on page 168.

LESSON 42

HE WENT ABOUT DOING GOOD

MATTHEW 4:23-25; ACTS 10:38

As Jesus ministered throughout the land of Galilee, he said and did things that left people amazed. His love and grace brought sinners to joy and the self-righteous to anger. To some he was a mystery, and to others he was Master.

Someone has wisely said, "As you study the Gospels, look for the glory of Christ." In the Bible, *glory* often means greatness or mighty power. One place the glory of Jesus is seen clearly is in the miracles he performed. They show us his amazing power and are signs that he truly is the Christ, the Son of the living God.

In the next series of lessons, we will look for the glory and power of Christ in some of his most well known miracles.

QUESTIONS:

1. True or false: Jesus' miracles prove that he is the Son of God.
2. In the Bible, _____ often means greatness or mighty power.
3. Where can we clearly see the glory of Christ in his ministry?
4. As you study the Gospels, look for
    (a) ways to get rich
    (b) secret codes
    (c) the glory of men
    (d) the glory of Christ
5. What kinds of people does Jesus love (lesson 29)?
6. Jesus said, "Repent, for the _____ is near!"

Answers on page 168.

49

PART IV

THE MIRACLES OF JESUS

LESSON 43

POWER OVER ALL THINGS

JOHN 20:29-31

When we are born, we get a birth certificate that serves as a record of who we are. It gives important information like our name, our mother's name, when and where we were born, and so on.

If Jesus had a birth certificate, it might say, "Jesus, the Son of God." But he didn't really need a certificate to prove who he was. His miracles were enough to prove he was the Son of God.

The Gospels record about thirty-four different miracles done by Jesus. There were many more, but these were enough to show that Jesus has absolute power over nature, sickness, demons, and even death. They are proof that the Kingdom of God has come and that Jesus is who he said he was—the Son of God.

QUESTIONS:

1. The miracles of Jesus are proof that he is
   - (a) a magician
   - (b) an actor
   - (c) the Son of God
   - (d) a good storyteller
2. About how many miracles do we find in the Gospels?
3. Name three things over which Jesus had absolute power.
4. True or false: Jesus' miracles were not a sign that the Kingdom of God had come.
5. True or false: Jesus did many more than thirty-four miracles.
6. In the Bible, _____ often means greatness or mighty power (lesson 42).

Answers on page 168.

LESSON 44

HEALING ALL WHO WERE UNDER THE POWER OF THE DEVIL

ACTS 10:38; MARK 5:1-19

In the gospel of Mark, we read of a man who lived in horrible misery. Many demons, the devil's servants, had made their home in him. He lived in tombs where the dead were buried, and night and day he would cry out in terrible pain. This poor man knew no love and had no hope until Jesus came to his rescue. When Jesus found him, he said, "Come out of that man, you unclean spirit!" (Mark 5:8). Within a few short moments, the demons were thrown out into a herd of pigs and the man was completely healed.

Demons were never a match for Jesus because he was filled with the Holy Spirit and with power. He was God's Messiah who came to set people free from the power of the devil.

QUESTIONS:

1. Jesus was God's Messiah who came to set people free from the power of the _____ .

2. The demons were thrown out into a herd of
    (a) cows
    (b) pigs
    (c) giraffes

3. True or false: Demons are the devil's servants.

4. The demon-possessed man knew no love or hope until _____ .

5. Why was Jesus able to defeat the devil and his demons?

6. True or false: The miracles of Jesus are proof that he is the Son of God.

Answers on page 169.

LESSON 45

THE MAN WITH THE SHRIVELED HAND

MARK 3:1-6

Jesus was a master teacher. On this day in the synagogue, he took the opportunity to use a man's shriveled, useless hand as a teaching tool. The lesson was clear: love and mercy are far more pleasing to God than strict, unbending rules.

The Pharisees thought it was wrong for Jesus to heal on the Sabbath day. They were watching to see what he would do so they could accuse him of breaking God's commandment to honor the Sabbath. Jesus knew this and he was angry and distressed at the stubbornness of their hearts. So right there in front of them he said to the man, "Stretch out your hand." Then he stretched his hand out, and it was completely healed.

Once again Jesus showed his power and glory. Once again proud people were furious at his goodness. And once again someone was rescued by the saving power of Immanuel.

QUESTIONS:

1. True or false: Love and mercy are far more pleasing to God than strict, legalistic rules.
2. True or false: The Pharisees thought it was good for Jesus to heal on the Sabbath.
3. Jesus was _____ at the stubbornness of the Pharisees.
4. The man's shriveled hand was completely _____ .
5. What name means "God with us"?

Answers on page 169.

LESSON 46

SIGHT TO THE BLIND

MARK 10:46-52

Unlike the proud Pharisees who rejected Jesus, those who trusted in him received the grace and blessing he came to give. Blind Bartimaeus was one of those people. Somehow he must have heard about Jesus' healing power, and when the opportunity came for him to get to Jesus, there was no stopping him!

As Jesus passed by, Bartimaeus cried out for mercy. Others told him to be quiet but true faith cannot be stopped so easily. He cried out even louder, "Son of David, have mercy on me!" (Mark 10:47). When Jesus called him, he threw his cloak aside, jumped to his feet, and made his way to him. With great excitement, Bartimaeus said to Jesus, "Rabbi, let me see again." Seeing his faith, Jesus restored his sight.

There is a great lesson to be learned here. Like Bartimaeus, we are all blinded by sin. Our selfishness keeps us from understanding how important Jesus is and how much we need his help. Therefore, we should not be content until we know the truth about Jesus and understand his place in our lives.

QUESTIONS:

1. True or false: Jesus came to bring blessing to others.
2. How did Bartimaeus feel about Jesus?
   (a) bored
   (b) not interested
   (c) excited
3. Blind Bartimaeus showed true _____ in Jesus.
4. What did Bartimaeus cry out?
5. Like Bartimaeus, we are all blinded by _____ .
6. True or false: Our selfishness keeps us from understanding how important Jesus is and how much we need his help.

Answers on page 169.

LESSON 47

WHAT KIND OF MAN IS THIS?

MATTHEW 8:23-27

The best we can do in the face of a horrible storm is find a safe place to hide until it passes. But on the Sea of Galilee, there is no place to hide.

Without warning, Jesus and his disciples found themselves in a terrible storm with the wind and waves about to swallow them up. In the midst of the chaos the disciples were filled with fear, but surprisingly, Jesus was fast asleep. In a panic they woke him up, not knowing what they were about to see. Then it happened. Jesus actually spoke to the wind and waves. He said, "Peace! Be still," and it became completely calm. The disciples could not believe their eyes.

Filled with amazement, they said, "What kind of man is this? Even the winds and the waves obey him!" Little by little they were learning that Jesus really was the Christ, the Son of the living God.

QUESTIONS:

1. When Jesus calmed the storm, what did the disciples ask one another?
2. Where was the disciples' boat when the storm came?
3. What did Jesus say to the wind and waves?
4. The disciples were
   - (a) sleepy
   - (b) bored
   - (c) amazed

   when Jesus calmed the storm.
5. True or false: Jesus was afraid during the storm.
6. What did Bartimaeus cry out?

Answers on page 169.

LESSON 48

BREAD FROM HEAVEN

JOHN 6:1-13, 35-51

If there were an Olympic Games for miracles, Jesus would win every medal in every event. His power to do the impossible is simply too great to imagine. Who else can use a little boy's lunch to feed five thousand men, plus the women and children?

But why did he do such amazing things? Was it just to fill a lot of hungry bellies for a day? Not quite.

Jesus used this particular miracle to show the crowds and the disciples that he is the true bread from Heaven that our souls need much more than food. His great miracles are meant to help us understand who he is and to cause us to love and cherish him above all other things.

QUESTIONS:

1. True or false: Jesus can do the impossible.
2. Jesus fed more than _____ people with one little boy's lunch.
3. Jesus is the true _____ from Heaven.
4. Jesus did miracles in order to
   (a) confuse people
   (b) impress others
   (c) show off his power
   (d) help us understand who he is
5. True or false: Jesus did not care if the crowds were hungry.

Answers on page 170.

LESSON 49

WATER INTO WINE

JOHN 2:1-11

The power Jesus has to change things is seen everywhere in the Gospels. He turns fishers of fish into fishers of men. He makes the sick well. He gives the blind sight. He puts a raging storm to sleep. He makes a shriveled hand whole. He makes the lame leap for joy. He makes the deaf hear and the dumb speak, and he also turns water into wine.

According to the Apostle John, this was no ordinary wine. It was the best wine these people had ever tasted. Jesus changed ordinary water into a drink fit for kings by the mere power of his will.

Such great power shows great glory. When his disciples saw his power and glory, they put their faith in him. So can we.

QUESTIONS:

1. What are some ways that Jesus showed his power to change things?

2. When his disciples saw his power, they put their _____ in him.

3. True or false: Jesus turned the water into wine by making a wish.

4. Jesus did miracles in order to

   (a) confuse people

   (b) to help us understand who he is

   (c) show off his power

   (d) impress others

5. When Jesus calmed the storm, what question did the disciples ask one another (lesson 47)?

Answers on page 170.

LESSON 50

THE STING OF DEATH

LUKE 7:11-17; EPHESIANS 2:1-3

A father's little girl, a widow's son, and a dear brother. Each different in many ways, but with one thing in common: they had all died. There was no heartbeat, no breath, nothing. Their lives were gone, and like a desert scorpion, death had left its painful sting in the hearts of their loved ones who were left behind. Like it always has, death brought pain and sadness, and they were powerless to do anything about it.

Death is the Bible's most often used picture of what we are all like apart from Jesus. We are born "dead in sin," meaning that because of sin in us, we can't know or please God. In that deadness we have no faith. We can't see God, and worst of all, we do not want to see or know Him.

But Jesus came to change that. As we will see in our next few lessons, Jesus came to set us free from the power of sin so we can know and serve the God who made us.

QUESTIONS:

1. Jesus comes to set us free from the power of sin so we can

    (a) be rich

    (b) play sports

    (c) know and serve the God who made us

2. True or false: The Bible says we are born "dead in sin."

3. Because of _____ we can't know or please God.

4. When his disciples saw Jesus' power, they put their _____ in him.

5. True or false: Jesus can do the impossible.

Answers on page 170.

LESSON 51

A FATHER AT THE FEET OF JESUS

MARK 5:22-24, 38-42

Jairus was an important man at the local synagogue, but now he was falling down at the feet of Jesus the great Rabbi. He begged Jesus, saying, "My little girl is dying. Please come put your hands on her so that she will be healed and live." Sadly, it was too late. Before Jesus got to her, she had taken her last breath. Her father's heart was broken—until Jesus began to do what only he can do.

Telling Jairus to trust him, Jesus found his daughter, took her hand and said, "Little girl, get up!" Immediately, she stood up and walked around.

With one command, Jesus defeated death and brought forth life. Her family would never forget the love and power Jesus showed them. That is exactly why he came—to bring love and life to the dead.

QUESTIONS:

1. Who wanted Jesus to heal his little girl?
2. True or false: The little girl died before Jesus got to her.
3. What did Jesus say to the little girl?
4. With one command, Jesus defeated _____ .
5. When his disciples saw Jesus' power, they put their _____ in him.

Answers on page 170.

LESSON 52

THE TENDER HEART OF JESUS

LUKE 7:11-17

She lived in a town called *Nain*, which means "pleasant." This day, however, was one of the saddest days of her life. Her son had died and was being carried out of the town to be buried. Little did she know what was about to happen.

As they passed through the gate of the town, Jesus was coming in. He saw the funeral and the woman weeping. Feeling her deep sadness, Jesus said to her, "Don't cry," and then he turned to the coffin and said to her dead son, "Young man, I say to you, get up!" In an instant the fellow came back to life and began to talk!

The crowds were struck by the sight and the woman must have been overcome with thankfulness. In only a moment, Jesus had lovingly turned her grief into joy, brought life to the dead, and revealed who he truly was—God, who had come to help His people.

QUESTIONS:

1. What does the word *Nain* mean?
2. When Jesus saw the woman weeping he
    (a) ignored her
    (b) told his disciples to care for her
    (c) stopped and cared for her himself
3. True or false: Jesus was God who had come to help His people.
4. Jesus came to bring love and life to the _____ (lesson 51).
5. What did Jesus say to the woman's son?

Answers on page 171.

L E S S O N   5 3

THE REASON FOR MIRACLES

JOHN 11:14-25, 40-42

Probably the hardest thing for any Christian is to trust in a God he cannot see. The Christian life is a call to follow someone who lived 2000 years ago. It is a life of holding on to an unseen hand. It is a life of faith—always trusting, always believing.

But even if we could see him, would we trust in him? The disciples were slow to trust and they walked with Jesus everyday for three years. So maybe the problem is not that we cannot see God. Maybe the problem is that we often choose to trust in ourselves instead of God.

Nevertheless, Jesus performed one of his greatest miracles—raising Lazarus from the dead—"so that you may believe," he told his disciples (John 11:15). It was a miracle they would never forget and Jesus made sure of it. He wanted them to trust in him and serve him faithfully, even in the worst of times.

God is still working miracles today. And even when He chooses not to perform a miracle, all we really need to know about His Son is written down for us in Scripture, so that we too may believe and trust in him.

QUESTIONS:

1. True or false: The Christian life is a life of faith and trusting in Jesus.
2. The disciples were
    (a) quick to trust Jesus
    (b) slow to trust Jesus
3. We often choose to trust in ourselves instead of _____ .
4. God has had all we need to know about His Son written down for us in
    (a) a magazine
    (b) the newspaper
    (c) the Bible
5. True or false: Jesus performed miracles so that we may be sure that he is the Son of God.
6. About how long ago did Jesus live?

Answers on page 171.

LESSON 54

LAZARUS

JOHN 11:11-15

"Our friend Lazarus has fallen asleep, and I am going there to wake him up," Jesus said (John 11:11, NIV). Actually, Lazarus was dead and Jesus knew it. He was going to do more than wake his friend up from sleep—he was going to wake him up from the dead.

This is one of the most glorious and exciting things about Jesus: he wakes the dead. He woke Jairus' little girl, the widow's son, and now his very own dear friend.

You may remember from lesson 50 that being someone without faith and trust in Jesus is like being dead. The Bible teaches us that we come into this world dead in sin, meaning that we are unwilling to love and trust Jesus. But the good news is that Jesus is still in the business of waking the dead. More about this in our next lesson.

QUESTIONS:

1. Jesus said, "Our friend Lazarus has fallen asleep, and I am going to _____ ."
2. What is one of the most glorious and exciting things about Jesus?
3. Name two people that Jesus brought back to life.
4. The Bible teaches that we come into this world

    (a) as basically good people

    (b) willing to love Jesus

    (c) dead in sin

5. Where do we learn about Jesus?
6. We often choose to trust in ourselves instead of _____ .

Answers on page 171.

LESSON 55

THE RESURRECTION AND THE LIFE

JOHN 5:24-25; JOHN 11:21-27

"I tell you the solemn truth, a time is coming—and is now here—when the dead will hear the voice of the Son of God, and those who hear will live," Jesus said (John 5:25). This is what the Bible calls *resurrection*. It is a power that causes dead people to come back to life. It is a power that only Jesus has. His voice alone can cause the dead to rise. In that way, he *is* the Resurrection.

Not only does he raise the dead, but he gives new life that will never end. Everyone who looks to Jesus and trusts in him for forgiveness of sin will have eternal life with him, and that new life begins the moment we look to him as our Savior.

When we trust in him, he gives himself to us for all eternity, and because he lives forever, so we will live forever with him. Therefore, as we read in the Scripture for this lesson, Jesus is both the Resurrection and the Life.

Has your soul heard his voice?

QUESTIONS:

1. Only _____ can cause the dead to rise.
2. Not only does Jesus raise the dead, he also gives them
   (a) a big house
   (b) eternal life
   (c) fancy clothes
3. True or false: Eternal life begins the moment we look to Jesus as our Savior.
4. Jesus said, "I am the _____ and the _____ ."

Answers on page 171.

LESSON 56

LAZARUS, COME OUT!

JOHN 11:38-44; EPHESIANS 2:4-5

Lazarus had been dead for four days and his body had begun to smell bad. Even so, Jesus gave orders to have the stone removed from the cave where he was buried. Looking to Heaven, he gave thanks to his Father for what was about to happen. Then in a loud voice Jesus cried, "Lazarus, come out!" Suddenly, Lazarus began to breathe and his heart began to beat. His eyes were opened and he walked out of the dark tomb alive and well.

This is the glory and greatness of Jesus on full display. He calls the dead by name and brings them to life. He is Lord over all things, even the grave, and he is still raising the dead. What does that mean? It means that people all over the world who trust in Jesus for forgiveness are being changed in their thoughts and feelings about him. The Bible calls this "being made alive." Their souls have heard his mighty voice, and just as he did for Lazarus, he also gives them a new life of knowing and loving God.

QUESTIONS:

1. How long had Lazarus been dead?
2. Looking to Heaven, Jesus gave _____ .
3. How did Jesus raise Lazarus from the dead?
4. True or false: Jesus said, "Lazarus, you may come out if you want."
5. Jesus is Lord over all things, even the _____ .
6. True or false: Whoever trusts in Jesus has eternal life.

Answers on page 172.

66

LESSON 57

AN AMAZING LACK OF FAITH

MARK 6:1-6

In the gospel of Mark, we are told of a time when Jesus was back in his hometown of Nazareth teaching in the synagogue. The people knew him but instead of praising him for his wisdom and power, they were offended at him. Mark writes, "He could not do any miracles there, except lay his hands on a few sick people and heal them. And he was amazed at their lack of faith" (Mark 6:5-6, NIV).

By rejecting Jesus as their Messiah, they cut themselves off from countless blessings. Jesus was able and willing, but the people in Nazareth were stubborn and unwilling to believe.

May it never be said of us that "he was amazed at their lack of faith."

QUESTIONS:

1. True or false: The people in Nazareth trusted in Jesus and believed in his miraculous power.

2. Jesus was amazed at their lack of _____ .

3. By rejecting Jesus, the people

    (a) were better off

    (b) missed out on many blessings

    (c) set a good example

4. True or false: The people in Nazareth were stubborn and unwilling to believe.

5. Jesus said to Martha, "I am the _____ and the Life" (lesson 55).

6. True or false: Whoever trusts in Jesus will never truly die.

Answers on page 172.

LESSON 58

UNREPENTANT

MATTHEW 11:20-24

The miracles of Jesus were not only meant to show us his power and glory. They were also meant to change our hearts and minds about him. That is what the Bible calls *repentance*—a change of how we think and feel about Jesus. Repentance is seeing his greatness, hearing his words, and then turning from sin and self to follow him. Repentance means that we receive Jesus as our Savior and King. We give ourselves to him and live to do his will. Repentance means that we turn *from* sin *to* Christ because knowing Christ is far better than anything sin could offer us.

Sadly, the cities where most of his miracles were done did not repent. They did not receive Jesus as Savior and worship him. Because of this, Jesus, like an Old Testament prophet, warned that Judgment Day would not be good for them.

As we look at the life of Jesus—hearing his words and seeing his power—let's not make that same mistake of remaining unrepentant.

QUESTIONS:

1. To repent means to change the way we _____ and _____ about Jesus.

2. True or false: Repentance is turning from sin and self to follow Jesus.

3. By rejecting Jesus, the people
   (a) were better off
   (b) missed out on many blessings
   (c) set a good example

4. True or false: God's Day of Judgment will be joyful for those who do not repent.

5. True or false: The people in Nazareth were stubborn and faithless.

Answers on page 172.

PART V

JESUS THE GREAT TEACHER

LESSON 59

YOU CALL ME TEACHER

MATTHEW 23:8; JOHN 13:13

Jesus is called "Teacher" about forty-five times in the Gospels. He is called *Rabbi*, the Aramaic word for "teacher," about fourteen times.

Jesus taught everywhere he went: in the synagogues, by the seaside, in the open fields and in the countryside. Unlike the Pharisees, he would teach anyone who would listen—including men, women, children, tax collectors, and the uneducated common folk. He especially taught his disciples, and later he would send them out to teach others.

QUESTIONS:

1. True or false: Jesus would only teach smart people.
2. Who would Jesus teach?
3. Name two places where Jesus would teach.
4. What does the word *rabbi* mean?
5. True or false: Jesus is called "Teacher" about forty-five times in the Gospels.
6. Jesus especially taught his disciples because later he would send them out to

    (a) teach others

    (b) play golf

    (c) get pizza

Answers on page 172.

LESSON 60

THE VERY WORDS OF GOD

JOHN 7:14-18; 12:49-50

The Jews were often amazed at Jesus and his teaching. Perhaps they forgot the words of Isaiah, that the Messiah would be "wonderful in counsel and magnificent in wisdom" (Isaiah 28:29, NIV). They said, "How does this man know so much when he has never had formal instruction?" He told them, "My teaching is not from me, but from the one who sent me." They were so shocked by his answer that they accused him of being possessed by a demon!

He told his disciples the same thing later on: "The words I say to you are not just my own...it is my Father, living within me, who is doing the work...these words belong to the Father who sent me...the Father who sent me commanded me what to say and how to say it...whatever I say is just what the Father has told me to say" (John 14:10; 12:49-50, NIV).

No wonder the Father said earlier, "Listen to him!" Jesus was sent *by* God to teach the world the truth *about* God. And his words were the very words *of* God.

QUESTIONS:

1. Jesus' words were not just his own, they were the _____ of God.
2. True or false: God sent His Son into the world.
3. True or false: The Jews believed that Jesus came from God to bring the truth.
4. Isaiah said that Jesus would be "magnificent in _____ ."
5. What does the word *rabbi* mean?
6. True or false: Jesus is called "Teacher" about six times in the Gospels.

Answers on page 173.

72

LESSON 61

THE TEACHER OF TEACHERS

JOHN 3:1-10

"Are you the teacher of Israel," said Jesus, "and yet you don't understand these things?" Nicodemus, a Pharisee, was receiving a gentle rebuke from the Master Teacher. Jesus often rebuked the Pharisees for not understanding the very Scriptures they claimed to love. He would say to them, "Have you not read this Scripture?" or "Are you not mistaken because you do not know the Scriptures?"

Jesus taught the very words of God and much of the time these words came straight from the Old Testament. As the Master Teacher, Jesus was a diligent and faithful student of those Scriptures. We have his example to follow here. Perhaps he would ask us the same question, "Have you not read this Scripture?"

Along with the Pharisees, the common people were always crowding around Jesus to hear him. Why? What was it that drew them in? In our next lessons, we will look at some of the things that drew people to his teaching.

QUESTIONS:

1. True or false: Jesus said to Nicodemus, "Are you the teacher of Israel, and yet you don't understand these things?"

2. As a Master Teacher, Jesus was a diligent and _____ student of the Scriptures.

3. Jesus taught the very words of _____ .

4. Jesus was "wonderful in counsel and magnificent in _____ "(lesson 60).

5. What does the word *rabbi* mean?

6. True or false: Jesus is called "Teacher" about forty-five times in the Gospels (lesson 59).

Answers on page 173.

LESSON 62

DRAWN BY GRACE

LUKE 5:1; 6:17; MATTHEW 7:28

A good teacher must know his lesson. But knowing the lesson is only a part of teaching. The teacher must also be able to speak in a way that draws the students into the lesson; otherwise, they will soon be daydreaming!

As a teacher, Jesus was full of grace. He made people feel welcome. He cared about his students. He was kind and gentle. His words were gracious, not sarcastic and mean. He gave himself to the tax collectors, the outcasts, the children, and they loved being with him. He was also filled with joy. Perhaps Jesus was laughing and smiling more than we might think. He also spoke with great authority and confidence. Often he would begin by saying, "I tell you the truth," or "I say to you." And don't forget, sometimes the lesson had a miracle to go with it, such as the man with the shriveled hand or the four thousand being fed!

All of these things demonstrate the fullness of grace that drew people to hear the Master.

QUESTIONS:

1. It was the _____ of Jesus that drew people to hear him teach.
2. True or false: Jesus taught with great authority and confidence.
3. Jesus taught the very words of _____ (lesson 60).
4. True or false: Jesus' words were often mean and sarcastic.
5. Jesus
    (a) didn't look at his students
    (b) was kind to his students
    (c) made his students feel dumb
6. Name three places where Jesus would often teach (lesson 59).

Answers on page 173.

LESSON 63

THE MASTER'S METHODS

MATTHEW 13:53-56

A master carpenter has lots of tools to work with. A master teacher has many tools as well. We know from our last lesson that Jesus' grace and kindness drew many people to hear his teaching. But there is more. They were not only drawn by who he was, they were also drawn by *how* he taught.

Jesus used many different tools to teach people about God. Some of his favorite tools were overstatement, hyperbole, similes and metaphors—as well as poetry, proverbs, and parables. Jesus used these tools to plant truth deep into the soil of peoples' hearts and minds. He used them to make what he said "sticky" and easy to remember.

We will look at each of these tools in our next lessons.

QUESTIONS:

1. True or false: Jesus wanted to make what he said "sticky" so people could remember what he taught them.
2. Name two tools Jesus used for teaching.
3. True or false: Jesus' grace and kindness drew many people to hear his teaching.
4. True or false: Jesus' words were often mean and sarcastic.
5. Jesus taught the very words of _____ (lesson 60).

Answers on page 173.

LESSON 64

OVERSTATEMENT

LUKE 14:26

Sometimes Jesus said things that sounded strange or even harsh in order to make his point clear. For example, instead of saying, "Be loyal and faithful to me at all times, no matter what," he said, "If anyone comes to me and does not hate his own father and mother, and wife and children, and brothers and sisters, and even his own life, he cannot be my disciple." The big question here is, what does he mean by "hate"?

We know Jesus does not want us to hate our parents or others. He wants us to love them. But by choosing this very strong word, Jesus uses *overstatement* to grab our attention and make his point. He wants us to see that our loyalty and devotion to him must be far greater than to anyone else. Ever.

QUESTIONS:

1. True or false: Jesus used overstatement to grab our attention and make his point clear.

2. Our _____ and devotion to Jesus is to be greater than to anyone else.

3. Jesus wants us to

    (a) ignore others

    (b) love others

    (c) make fun of others

4. True or false: Overstatement made what Jesus taught "sticky" so that we would remember what he said.

Answers on page 174.

LESSON 65

HYPERBOLE

MATTHEW 7:1-5

Jesus wanted to teach people about their sin and he was often very creative in the way he did it. For example, rather than saying, "Pay attention to your own faults and sins before pointing out the faults of others," Jesus said, "Why do you see the speck in your brother's eye, but fail to see the beam of wood in your own? First remove the beam from your own eye." This way of speaking is called *hyperbole* (high-PURR-bo-lee). No one's eye is big enough to have a log or beam of wood in it, but our sins and faults are big enough that we should see them long before we see the faults and sins of others. That is what Jesus wants us to see.

Hyperbole uses extreme exaggeration, such as a log being in a person's eye, people swallowing camels, camels fitting into the eye of a needle, and left hands hiding from right hands. These are all examples of hyperbole in the teachings of Jesus.

QUESTIONS:

1. Taking a log out of your eye is an example of

    (a) poetry

    (b) dance

    (c) hyperbole

2. True or false: We should pay attention to our own sins before we point out the sins of others.

3. Give another example of hyperbole that Jesus used.

4. True or false: Hyperbole helped Jesus make his teaching "sticky" so we could easily remember what he said.

5. Hyperbole uses extreme _____ .

Answers on page 174.

LESSON 66

SIMILE

MATTHEW 23:27-28

Some things can be very different yet very much alike. A person is nothing like a tomb. One is living and the other is a place for the dead. Using a *simile* (SIM-uh-lee), Jesus said the Pharisees were like "whitewashed tombs." How were they alike? Well, Jesus explains this himself. He told them, "You are *like* whitewashed tombs that look beautiful on the outside but inside are full of the bones of the dead and of everything unclean. In the same way, on the outside you look righteous to people, but inside you are full of hypocrisy and lawlessness."

On another occasion, Jesus told his disciples to be "wise *as* serpents, but innocent *as* doves" (Matthew 10:16). This is a simile that compares people to serpents and doves.

Notice that a simile uses the words *like* or *as* to compare things. Jesus used this tool many times in his teaching.

QUESTIONS:

1. A sentence that uses *like* or *as* to compare things is called a _____ .
2. Jesus said the Pharisees were like whitewashed _____ .
3. In what way were the Pharisees like whitewashed tombs?
4. True or false: Taking a log out of your eye is an example of hyperbole.
5. What three teaching tools have we looked at so far?

Answers on page 174.

LESSON 67

METAPHOR

MATTHEW 7:15

Jesus could have said, "Watch out for false prophets, because they will try to trick you." But instead, he used a much more colorful way of speaking: "They come to you in sheep's clothing, but inwardly they are ferocious wolves." A sentence that compares things this way—saying that false prophets *are* ferocious wolves—is known as a *metaphor*. Some of Jesus' most famous sayings are metaphors. "You *are* the light of the world" (Matthew 5:14). "I *am* the Bread of Life" (John 6:48). "This *is* my body which is broken for you" (First Corinthians 11:24, NKJV).

A metaphor uses one thing to describe another—the way Jesus uses wolves to describe the Pharisees, light to describe true disciples, and bread to describe his own body. This is yet another way Jesus made his words easy to remember.

QUESTIONS:

1. True or false: A metaphor uses one thing to describe another.
2. True or false: The sentence "You are like whitewashed tombs" is an example of a metaphor.
3. What are some famous metaphors that Jesus used?
4. False prophets come in sheep's clothing, but inwardly they are _____ .
5. True or false: "You are a whitewashed tomb" is an example of a metaphor.

Answers on page 174.

LESSON 68

THE POETRY OF JESUS

LUKE 11:9-11

Poetry is a wonderful teaching tool that Jesus loved to use. As a boy, he learned the language of poetry from the Psalms, Proverbs, and Prophets. His poetic style of teaching was filled with word pictures and repetition. Like the other tools we have looked at so far, Jesus used poetry to help people understand and remember what he taught.

Jesus once painted a picture of prayer that we could never forget:

> Ask and it will be given to you;
> seek and you will find;
> knock and the door will be opened to you.
> For everyone who asks receives;
> he who seeks finds;
> and to him who knocks, the door will be opened.

This is the poetry of Jesus.

QUESTIONS:

1. Jesus learned the language of poetry from the _____ , _____ , and _____ .

2. True or false: Jesus' teachings were filled with word pictures and repetition.

3. Poetry makes Jesus' teaching
   (a) hard to remember
   (b) easy to remember

4. True or false: "I am the Door" is a metaphor.

5. Why did Jesus teach with poetry?

Answers on page 175.

LESSON 69

PROVERBS

MATTHEW 6:34

In the game of darts, you take a short, straight shaft with a sharp point and throw it at a round target. The goal is to get your dart to stick as closely as possible to the center of the target, called the "bullseye." Much like that dart, a proverb is a short sentence that is meant to make a point or teach a lesson.

We find proverbs everywhere in the Gospels. Here are just a few examples: "Where your treasure is, there your heart will be also," "You cannot serve God and money," and "Do not worry about tomorrow, for tomorrow will worry about itself." Jesus crafted these and many more proverbs, and with expert skill he aimed for the bullseye—the hearts and minds of those he taught.

QUESTIONS:

1. True or false: A proverb is a short sentence that is meant to make a point or teach a lesson.

2. Jesus said, "Where your _____ is, there your _____ will be also."

3. Jesus learned the language of poetry from the _____ , _____ , and _____ .

4. True or false: Jesus taught people with word pictures, repetition, and proverbs.

5. Give an example of one of Jesus' proverbs.

Answers on page 175.

L E S S O N 7 0

PARABLES

MATTHEW 13:34-35

Of all the tools Jesus used for teaching, the parable seems to have been his favorite. There are at least forty different parables in the Gospels, not including the gospel of John. A parable is a short story that Jesus would tell to illustrate a teaching about the Kingdom. These stories used things from everyday life such as seeds, coins, and sheep to teach about the Kingdom of God and the Father's love.

Jesus wanted people to find themselves in the stories he told. He also wanted them to see something about the Kingdom of God or about God Himself. Last but not least, he wanted to move people to action—to do something because of what he was teaching in the parables.

QUESTIONS:

1. The gospels of Matthew, Mark, and Luke include at least how many parables?
2. True or false: A parable is a short story that uses things from ordinary life to make a point.
3. Name three things Jesus used in his parables.
4. Name two things Jesus would teach about using parables.
5. True or false: Jesus wanted people to see themselves and the Kingdom of God in the parables.

Answers on page 175.

LESSON 71

UNDERSTANDING PARABLES

MATTHEW 13:1-9, 18-23

As you read and study the parables, keep one question in mind: *What is the main point of this parable?* This question will help you see what Jesus wanted to teach his listeners.

For example, in the parable of the sower the person who hears about the Kingdom is being compared to different types of soil, and only one is able to bear fruit for the Kingdom of God. The main point is this: what we do with the message of the Kingdom is determined by our willingness to love that Kingdom more than anything else.

In the next few lessons we will explore the most famous of parables: the parable of the prodigal son.

QUESTIONS:

1. What question will help you understand the parables?

2. True or false: What we do with the message of the Kingdom is determined by our willingness to love that Kingdom more than anything else.

3. A parable is a short story that uses ordinary things to make

   (a) a point

   (b) an apology

   (c) a pizza

4. Name one thing that Jesus would often teach about by using parables.

5. True or false: Jesus wanted people to see themselves and the Kingdom of God in the parables.

Answers on page 175.

LESSON 72

THE PRODIGAL SON

LUKE 15:1-32

Remember that Jesus used certain parables for certain situations. This parable came about because Jesus was spending time with sinners, and the Pharisees did not like it. Although the parable of the prodigal (wasteful) son has much to teach us, the main point was to show the Pharisees how unlike the Father they really were and that God loves tax collectors and sinners.

Now that we know the main point of the parable, we will look next at its main characters: the father and his two sons.

QUESTIONS:

1. Jesus used certain _____ for certain _____ .
2. True or false: The Pharisees thought it was wonderful that Jesus spent time with sinners.
3. What is the main point of the parable of the prodigal son?
4. Who are the three main characters in the parable?
5. Jesus was full of _____ and truth (lesson 22).

Answers on page 176.

LESSON 73

THE YOUNGER BROTHER

LUKE 15:11-24

Jesus begins his story with the younger brother leaving his father's house. It seems the young fellow wanted to make up his own rules and live however he pleased. Then, when he finds out how miserable life is apart from his father, the prodigal son repents, makes the journey home, and seeks his father's forgiveness. "Father, I have sinned against Heaven and against you. I am no longer worthy to be called your son," he says.

This was a picture of the tax collectors and sinners who saw their need for Jesus and came back to God the Father. Like them, we can also find ourselves in this story—either running from the Father or coming back to Him.

QUESTIONS:

1. In this parable, who is most like the younger brother, the Pharisees or the tax collectors and sinners?

2. When he finds out how miserable life is apart from his father, the son repents, makes the journey home, and seeks his father's

   (a) camel

   (b) money

   (c) forgiveness

3. True or false: The younger brother did the right thing by leaving his father.

4. True or false: The main point of this parable is to show the Pharisees how unlike the Father they really were (lesson 72).

5. What question will help you understand the parables of Jesus?

Answers on page 176.

L E S S O N   7 4

THE FATHER

LUKE 15:11-20

The younger brother was selfish and proud. He wasted all his father had given him. But when he could go no lower in his misery, he realized how foolish he was and started back home to his father. Then we read, "while he was still a long way off, his father saw him and was filled with compassion for him; he ran to his son, threw his arms around him, and kissed him" (Luke 15:20, NIV).

What the father did revealed the heart of God and the hearts of the Pharisees. They were very different. The Pharisees had no use for repentant sinners, but as Jesus' story unfolds, it becomes clear that the Father is not a Pharisee.

QUESTIONS:

1. True or false: When the younger brother came back home, the father hid from him.

2. What did the father do when he saw his son?

3. True or false: The Pharisees had a great love for tax collectors and sinners.

4. The younger brother did the

   (a) right thing

   (b) wrong thing

   by coming back home.

5. What question will help you understand the parables of Jesus (lesson 71)?

Answers on page 176.

LESSON 75

THE ELDER BROTHER

LUKE 15:25-32

In the parable of the prodigal son, Jesus uses the elder brother to show the Pharisees their true attitude toward God. He was proud, bitter, and unwilling to trust in the goodness and mercy of his father. He said that living with his father was a life of joyless slavery. "These many years I have worked like a slave for you," he said.

Like the elder brother, the Pharisees did not trust that God was good and merciful, and that He joyfully welcomes sinners. We all tend to see God this way, but that is wrong. Jesus said, "The person who has seen me has seen the Father" (John 14:9). Jesus was not the Father, but he was *like* the Father in his love for sinners. Let us always look to the Lord Jesus and see what the elder brother and Pharisees did not see: the goodness and mercy of the Father.

QUESTIONS:

1. Jesus uses the elder brother in the parable to show the Pharisees

    (a) how wonderful they were

    (b) how righteous they were

    (c) how wrong they were

2. True or false: The elder brother did not trust in the goodness of his father.

3. Jesus said, "The person who has seen me has seen _____ .''

4. The younger brother did the

    (a) right thing

    (b) wrong thing

    by coming back home.

5. We should always look to Jesus and see the goodness and _____ of the Father.

Answers on page 176.

PART VI

JESUS AND THE KINGDOM OF GOD

LESSON 76

THE KINGDOM OF GOD

MARK 1:14-15

Every good recipe has one or two ingredients that make it special. The teaching ministry of Jesus had a few choice ingredients as well. By far, the main ingredient in his teaching was the *Kingdom of God*. Jesus was always talking about the Kingdom of God. He spoke about the Kingdom of God more than the love of God. In fact, the words "Kingdom of God" or "Kingdom of Heaven" are used at least sixty-one times in the Gospels.

Luke says that Jesus was sent to proclaim the good news of the Kingdom of God. Jesus even began his ministry with these famous words, "The time is fulfilled and the Kingdom of God is near. Repent and believe the gospel!"

QUESTIONS:

1. True or false: The main theme of Jesus' teaching was the love of God.

2. The main theme of Jesus' teaching was the _____ .

3. True or false: The words "Kingdom of God" or "Kingdom of Heaven" are used at least sixty-one times in the Gospels.

4. Luke says that Jesus was sent to proclaim the _____ of the Kingdom of God.

5. Jesus was always talking about

    (a) how to get rich

    (b) how to be a better person

    (c) the Kingdom of God

Answers on page 177.

LESSON 77

TWO NAMES, ONE KINGDOM

MATTHEW 19:23-24

In the Gospels, Matthew uses the words "Kingdom of Heaven," but Mark, Luke, and John use "Kingdom of God." Why? Are there two different kingdoms? Not really.

Matthew uses "Kingdom of Heaven" because he wrote his gospel mainly for Jewish people, and they had such a reverence and respect for the name of God that many would not even say it. They did not want to break the third Commandment by misusing God's holy name.

So, for this reason, Matthew used the word "Heaven" instead of "God." We know they mean the same thing because Matthew would sometimes use both expressions in the same passage, as the Scripture for this lesson shows.

QUESTIONS:

1. Matthew often used the word _____ instead of "God."

2. True or false: The Jewish people had a great reverence for God's name and many would not even say it.

3. True or false: The "Kingdom of Heaven" and "Kingdom of God" are speaking about the same Kingdom.

4. The main theme of Jesus' teaching was the _____ (lesson 76).

5. Mark, Luke, and John use the words "Kingdom of _____ ."

6. True or false: The Jewish people did not want to break the third Commandment.

Answers on page 177.

LESSON 78

THE ETERNAL KINGDOM

PSALM 145:10-13

The Kingdom of God is not all that new. In fact, it has been around for as long as God Himself. He is the eternal King, with no beginning and no ending. And as is the King, so is the Kingdom—eternal and without end.

The prophet Isaiah said, "of the increase of his government...there will be no end" (Isaiah 9:7, NIV). Jesus said that the Kingdom of God is like a mustard seed, small at first, but eventually becoming the largest of all plants. In other words, it is always growing and becoming greater than all other kingdoms.

After all the kingdoms of the world have faded away, God's Kingdom alone will remain, and it will never end.

QUESTIONS:

1. True or false: The Kingdom of God stopped growing long ago.
2. Which prophet said, "of the increase of his government...there will be no end?"
3. God is the eternal King, with no beginning and no _____ .
4. The main theme of Jesus' teaching was the _____ .
5. Jesus was always talking about
    (a) how to get rich
    (b) how to be a better person
    (c) the Kingdom of Heaven

Answers on page 177.

LESSON 79

WHERE GOD'S WILL IS DONE

MATTHEW 6:9-10

The word *kingdom* is a short form of "domain of the king," or "king's dominion." A domain is the place where the glory and power of the king is found. It is the place where the will of the king is carried out.

This is how Jesus explains the Kingdom of God. In the Lord's Prayer, he says we should pray, "Your Kingdom come, your *will* be done, on earth as it is in Heaven."

God's Kingdom is found wherever His will is being done.

QUESTIONS:

1. God's Kingdom is found wherever His _____ is being done.
2. True or false: We should always pray for God's will to be done.
3. What two words combined make the word "kingdom?"
4. True or false: A domain is the place where the glory and power of the king is found.
5. A kingdom is where the _____ of the king is being done.
6. God is the eternal King, with no _____ and no _____ (lesson 78).

Answers on page 177.

LESSON 80

A CITIZEN OF THE KINGDOM

MATTHEW 5:3; 6:33; 7:21

Like earthly kingdoms or nations, those who belong to the Kingdom of God are called to live by the rules of the Kingdom. They are called to do the will of the King and to seek His glory first above all things. However, Jesus taught that not everyone who says he belongs to God's Kingdom is really a citizen of the Kingdom.

He says that only those who do "the will of my Father" belong to the Kingdom. They are the ones who are humble, poor in spirit, and care about being truly righteous, not proud pretenders like the Pharisees. Members of God's Kingdom do not trust in their own goodness but they depend completely upon the mercy and goodness of the King as they do His will.

QUESTIONS:

1. According to Jesus, only those who do _____ belong to the Kingdom.

2. True or false: True Kingdom citizens do not trust in their own goodness, but they depend upon the goodness of the King.

3. True or false: We should always pray for God's will to be done.

4. A Kingdom citizen is

    (a) a proud pretender

    (b) a basically good person

    (c) someone who does the will of God and seeks His glory

5. A kingdom is where the _____ of the king is being done.

6. Which prophet said, "of the increase of his government there will be no end" (lesson 78)?

Answers on page 178.

LESSON 81

NOW AND NOT YET

LUKE 22:14-18

Sometimes, Jesus would speak of seeing the Kingdom, entering the Kingdom, or seeking the Kingdom. Other times he would say things like "Your Kingdom come" or "until the Kingdom of God comes." This might seem a bit confusing. Had the Kingdom really come or not? Well, yes and no.

In one sense, the Kingdom of God has come, and in another way, it is still yet to come. It is present and future. Now and not yet. Like Jesus said in the mustard seed parable, the Kingdom is growing silently but surely. One day it will be the one and only eternal Kingdom where Jesus will reign forever and ever.

QUESTIONS:

1. The Kingdom of God is now and _____ .
2. True or false: Jesus taught that God's Kingdom is no longer growing.
3. The Kingdom is both present and _____ .
4. A Kingdom citizen is
    (a) a proud pretender
    (b) a basically good person
    (c) someone who does the will of God and seeks His glory
5. According to Jesus, only those who do _____ belong to the Kingdom.

Answers on page 178.

LESSON 82

THE NOW KINGDOM

MARK 1:14-15; LUKE 11:14-20

Alarm clocks are wonderful tools. They let us know when it is time to wake up and get started with our day. When Jesus came, he was like an alarm clock. At the beginning of his ministry, he said, "the time is fulfilled, and the Kingdom of God is at hand!" He was saying, "Wake up! The time has come! The Kingdom is here!" When he came, so did the Kingdom.

Everywhere he went you could see the Kingdom—the rule and reign of God. When demons were cast out, when the blind began to see, and when the crippled began to walk, the will of God was being done and the Kingdom of God was there.

Jesus' call for sinners to repent and give themselves to him as their King opened the door for people of every nation to enter the Kingdom of God. That door is still open and the Kingdom of God is still at hand.

QUESTIONS:

1. When Jesus came, so did the _____ .

2. Jesus said, "The _____ is fulfilled, and the _____ of God is at hand."

3. True or false: When demons were cast out and people were healed, the will of God was being done.

4. The gospel calls us to

    (a) be good people so that we can go to Heaven

    (b) repent and give ourselves to Jesus

    (c) wait until we are old to follow Jesus

5. True or false: Only good people are invited to enter the Kingdom.

Answers on page 178.

LESSON 83

THE KINGDOM YET TO COME

MATTHEW 6:9-13; 25:1-13

In the "Lord's Prayer," Jesus taught that the Kingdom of God is still to come. He said, "May your kingdom come, may your will be done on earth as it is in heaven." We know that God's will is not fully done on earth as it is in Heaven because of all the bad things that are a part of this world such as sin, suffering, disease, and death. So, Jesus said to pray for the day to come when the Father's will is done in every place and in every way.

The parables also teach us that the Kingdom of Heaven is yet to come. The parable of the ten virgins (Matthew 25:1-13) warns of the future return of Christ. The main point of the parable is that we should be ready and waiting for him, because when Christ the Bridegroom comes, so will the Kingdom.

QUESTIONS:

1. When Christ the Bridegroom comes, so will the _____ .

2. True or false: The parables often teach us that the Kingdom of God is yet to come.

3. What did Jesus tell us to pray for?

4. The gospel calls us to

    (a) be good people so that we can go to Heaven

    (b) repent and give ourselves to Jesus

    (c) wait until we are old to follow Jesus

5. How do we know that God's will is not being fully done in the world?

6. One day, all earthly kingdoms will end and _____ will reign forever and ever (lesson 81).

Answers on page 178.

LESSON 84

THE KINGDOM OF HEAVEN IS THE TREASURE

MATTHEW 13:44

Wherever you are right now, take a moment to look around. Probably everything you see cost someone some amount of money. The house you live in, the clothes you wear, and the wonderful things you may have are worth a lot to you; they are important to you. They have what we call *value*.

Jesus wants us to know that his Kingdom is worth more than all we have. It is worth more than all the money and things in the world. The Kingdom of God is the greatest treasure and it brings the greatest joy.

The parable of the hidden treasure is about the value of the Kingdom, and it asks us this question: What is most important to us? Is it all the stuff we have, or knowing the King and doing His will?

QUESTIONS:

1. What is the parable of the hidden treasure about?

2. The Kingdom of God is worth more than _____ .

3. The Kingdom of Heaven brings us

    (a) lots of money

    (b) lots of joy

    (c) good luck

4. What did Jesus tell us to pray for (lesson 83)?

5. True or false: Kingdom citizens do not trust in their own goodness, but they depend upon the goodness of the King (lesson 80).

6. Name three ways that we know God's will is not being fully done in the world (lesson 83).

7. What is most important to you?

Answers on page 179.

PART VII

JESUS AND LIFE IN THE KINGDOM

LESSON 85

GOD LOOKS UPON THE HEART

MATTHEW 5:20

The religious leaders had fallen into a terrible trap. At first, they sought to be truly righteous, but over time their hearts became hard and proud. They began to focus only on the outside and keeping lots of rules like washing hands and doing absolutely nothing on the Sabbath. All the while, they became mean and miserable on the inside.

However, the common people still thought the religious leaders were very righteous. Imagine their surprise when Jesus said, "Your righteousness must be greater than the scribes and Pharisees, or you can never enter the kingdom" (NIV). They may have thought, "How could we *ever* be more righteous than the Pharisees?" According to Jesus, they needed to realize that true righteousness is found in having the right heart attitude and not simply keeping a list of rules.

God looks upon the attitude of our hearts—how we think and feel about God, ourselves, and others—and the Sermon on the Mount (found in chapters 5-7 of the gospel of Matthew) tells us just what He is looking for. That will be the focus of our next series of lessons.

QUESTIONS:

1. True or false: The religious leaders cared more about keeping lots of rules than about the attitude of their hearts.

2. Why were people surprised when Jesus said they must be more righteous than the scribes and Pharisees?

3. The Pharisees started out well, but over time their hearts became hard and _____ .

4. Jesus said, "Your righteousness must be greater than the scribes and Pharisees, or you can never enter the _____ ."

5. True or false: The Kingdom of Heaven is worth more than all we have.

6. The gospel calls us to
    (a) try to be good enough to go to Heaven
    (b) repent and give ourselves to Jesus
    (c) wait until we are old to follow Jesus

Answers on page 179.

LESSON 86

CLEAN HANDS AND A PURE HEART

PSALM 24:3-5

Much of Jesus' teaching came from his understanding of the Old Testament Scriptures. In fact, the first part of the Sermon on the Mount sounds a lot like Psalm 24, which connects a pure heart with blessing. Jesus begins by telling the people about God's blessing upon the righteous. He tells them what true goodness and righteousness looks like. He says that the one who is truly happy is the one who is truly holy.

Jesus tells us that God is holy and that He intends for His children to become like Him. As we study the Sermon on the Mount, we find that becoming like God means a life long journey of being made clean and pure in our thoughts, words, and deeds.

QUESTIONS:

1. True or false: In the Sermon on the Mount, Jesus taught about God's blessing upon the righteous.

2. Jesus also teaches the people what true _____ looks like.

3. The one who is truly happy is the one who is truly _____ .

4. True or false: Jesus teaches us that God is holy and that He intends for His children to be like Him.

5. How does God want us to be clean and pure?

6. Being righteous will make us

   (a) happy

   (b) worried

   (c) sad

Answers on page 179.

LESSON 87

POOR IN SPIRIT

MATTHEW 5:3

In our world the goal is to become rich, but in the Kingdom of God the goal is to become poor. Not poor in terms of money and things, but *poor in spirit*. Jesus says that those who are poor in spirit have everything—they have the Kingdom. But what does it mean to be "poor in spirit?"

The person who knows there is nothing good in himself apart from the goodness of God has become poor in spirit. He has seen himself to be a lost sinner in need of mercy and grace. He is like the prodigal son with nothing to boast or brag about and nothing to bring to the Father. All he has is faith in Jesus and complete dependence upon the mercy of God.

This is the one who is truly rich and truly happy. Is that you?

QUESTIONS:

1. "Blessed are the poor in spirit, for the _____ belongs to them."

2. True or false: In order to become poor in spirit, you must give all your possessions away.

3. True or false: In order to become poor in spirit, you must see yourself as a sinner in need of God's mercy.

4. A proud and boastful person

    (a) is poor in spirit

    (b) is not poor in spirit

5. Jesus' sermon tells us that God is holy and He intends for His children to be _____ .

6. Where in the Bible will you find the Sermon on the Mount?

Answers on page 179.

LESSON 88

THOSE WHO MOURN

MATTHEW 5:4; PSALM 34:18; 147:3

It is one thing to say, "I'm sorry," but it is another thing altogether to *be sorrowful* when we have done something wrong. Those who mourn are sorry for the sin they have committed against God. They have felt the awfulness of their own sin and are very sorry for what they have done.

Again, the prodigal son is a perfect example. Like him, those who mourn say to God, "I am not worthy to be your son." Then God comforts them with mercy and forgiveness. The Father welcomes them, makes them His children, and loves them beyond measure.

QUESTIONS:

1. How are those who mourn comforted?

2. The prodigal son said, "I am not _____ to be your son."

3. True or false: Those who mourn are sorry because they got caught doing something wrong.

4. Those who mourn are sorry for the sin they have committed against _____ .

5. A proud and boastful person

    (a) is poor in spirit

    (b) is not poor in spirit

6. Where in the Bible will you find the Sermon on the Mount?

Answers on page 180.

LESSON 89

BLESSED ARE THE MEEK

MATTHEW 5:5; PSALM 37:1-11

Someone has said that meekness is a jewel polished by grace. It sparkles like a diamond cut to perfection. And like that diamond, meekness is a rare thing indeed.

No doubt Jesus had Psalm 37 in mind when he spoke the words we read in Matthew 5:5. In that Psalm the meek are described as those who wait patiently for the Lord and trust in Him to work all things together for their good. God is enough for them, so they are not angry when bad things happen to them and good things happen to those who ignore God.

Under their Father's guidance, those who are meek learn patience and submission to His will. Jesus is our great example as we seek to become those who will one day inherit the earth.

QUESTIONS:

1. What Psalm teaches us about being meek?

2. Under their Father's guidance, the meek learn _____ and submission to His will.

3. True or false: A meek person demands his own way and gets angry when good things happen to others.

4. How are those who mourn comforted (lesson 88)?

5. In order to become poor in spirit, you must see yourself as a sinner in need of God's _____ (lesson 87).

6. Jesus said, "Your righteousness must be greater than the scribes and Pharisees, or you can never enter the _____ " (lesson 85).

Answers on page 180.

LESSON 90

HUNGRY AND THIRSTY

MATTHEW 5:6; PSALM 107:1-9

When our bellies are empty and our mouths are dry as dust, we will stop at nothing until we find relief. These feelings remind us that food and water are two things we cannot live without.

Jesus says his disciples feel that way about righteousness. They are not happy unless they have a right relationship with God and others. They want a life that is marked by righteousness—doing what pleases their heavenly Father. Their hearts hunger for these things like someone who is starving for food.

And this is the promise they receive from Jesus: they will be filled. As they want what only God can give, He will indeed give it to them. He satisfies the longing soul and the hungry soul He fills with good things.

QUESTIONS:

1. Name two things we cannot live without.

2. Name two things a disciple of Jesus cannot be happy without.

3. True or false: A disciple of Jesus does not care about having a right relationship with others.

4. Jesus said, "Blessed are those who hunger and thirst for righteousness, for they will be _____ ."

5. Under the Father's guidance, the meek learn patience and submission to his _____ .

6. A proud and boastful person
    (a) is poor in spirit
    (b) is not poor in spirit

Answers on page 180.

LESSON 91

MERCY IN, MERCY OUT

MATTHEW 5:7; HOSEA 6:6; EXODUS 34:6

Imagine being in a restaurant waiting for your food. You see the waiter coming to your table with a cup in his hand. Then someone walks by, bumps into the server, and suddenly what was in the cup is now all over your clothes! Jesus says our hearts are like that cup. When it gets bumped, whatever is in the cup is going to spill out.

Sometimes others "bump" into us, so to speak. They say hurtful things, do mean things, or mistreat us. But, if our hearts are filled with God's mercy and forgiveness, then mercy and forgiveness will come out.

Being merciful does not earn God's mercy, but it does show that we belong to Jesus and that he is making us more like himself.

QUESTIONS:

1. True or false: Being merciful and forgiving shows that we belong to Jesus.

2. If mercy is in our hearts, then

    (a) anger

    (b) forgiveness

    (c) harsh words

    will come out.

3. Give two ways others may "bump" into us.

4. Exodus 34:6 says the Lord is a merciful and gracious God, slow to _____ , and abounding in steadfast _____ .

5. True or false: A disciple of Jesus does not care about having a right relationship with others.

6. Jesus said, "Blessed are those who hunger and thirst for righteousness, for they will be _____ ."

Answers on page 180.

LESSON 92

A GOOD KIND OF STUBBORN

MATTHEW 5:8; PSALM 24:1-5

According to Psalm 24, being pure in heart has to do with not lifting up your soul to an idol or a false god. That means trusting in God alone to provide all you need, since all the world is His. It means you are willing to stand alone when everyone else turns away from Jesus. You have pledged your allegiance to him and have a devotion that is stubborn and unwilling to trust in an idol.

This is one kind of stubbornness that will bring you great happiness and eternal reward. You will see God. Those who cling to Jesus and trust in him alone will dwell in the presence of absolute purity and holiness for all eternity. Jesus said, "Blessed are the pure in heart, for they will see God."

QUESTIONS:

1. True or false: The pure in heart will see God and dwell in His presence for all eternity.

2. Being devoted to Christ means being unwilling to trust in an _____ .

3. What Psalm tells us about having a pure heart?

4. A pure heart trusts in

   (a) money

   (b) knowledge

   (c) the government

   (d) Christ alone

5. True or false: Being merciful and forgiving shows that we belong to Jesus.

6. If mercy is in our hearts, then

   (a) anger

   (b) forgiveness

   (c) harsh words

   will come out.

Answers on page 181.

LESSON 93

BLESSED ARE THE PEACEMAKERS

MATTHEW 5:9; PSALM 34:11-14

There is an old saying, "like father, like son." It means that children bear the *image* of their parents. Children are like their parents in many ways. Someone might say, "you look just like your dad," or "you have your mother's eyes."

In the same way, God's children bear His *image*, and over time they become more and more like him—not in the way they look, but in the way they think and feel about things. God's children begin to do what God Himself would do. He provides their peace and blessing, and they seek that same peace and blessing for others. The Father shows love and care for His children, and the children reflect that love and care by the way they love and care for those around them.

Therefore, Jesus says, "Blessed are the peacemakers, for they will be called the children of God."

QUESTIONS:

1. True or false: Many children look like their parents.

2. God's children bear the _____ of their heavenly Father.

3. Being a peacemaker means

   (a) liking to argue

   (b) being quiet all of the time

   (c) seeking peace and blessing for others

4. Jesus said, "Blessed are the peacemakers for they shall be called _____ ."

5. Being devoted to Christ means being unwilling to trust in an _____ .

6. True or false: In order to become poor in spirit, you must give all your possessions away (lesson 87).

Answers on page 181.

L E S S O N 9 4

PERSECUTED? REJOICE AND BE GLAD

MATTHEW 5:10-11

While Jesus teaches that happiness lives next door to holiness, he also says don't expect everyone to approve of how you live for him! He knows firsthand that this sinful world does not give his disciples a standing ovation. He warns that quite the opposite may happen.

Children of the kingdom will be made fun of, talked about, ignored, and falsely accused of doing wrong. These, Jesus says, are signs that we are really citizens of another Kingdom. They remind us that we belong not to this world but to the glorious world to come, where righteousness will reign forever. If we have taken Jesus as Savior, that Kingdom is ours. Therefore, we have every reason to rejoice and leap for joy when others reject us because we belong to Jesus.

QUESTIONS:

1. Jesus said, "Blessed are those who are persecuted for righteousness sake, for the Kingdom of _____ belongs to them."

2. What are some ways others may mistreat us because we seek to live a holy life?

3. True or false: When others make fun of us for serving Jesus, we should get angry and speak harshly to them.

4. Being a peacemaker means

    (a) liking to argue

    (b) being quiet all of the time

    (c) seeking peace and good for others

5. In the glorious world to come, _____ will reign forever.

6. What Psalm tells us about having a pure heart (lesson 86)?

Answers on page 181.

LESSON 95

SALT OF THE EARTH

MATTHEW 5:13

After showing his disciples what Kingdom happiness looks like, Jesus now tells them how God intends to bless the world through their witness. Using a simple metaphor, he says, "You are the salt of the earth."

Like salt, most of Jesus' followers seem little and unimportant, but it is through them that the world gets a taste of the goodness of God. They bring the flavor of mercy and peace to a world made bitter by sin.

Jesus also says that his followers must remain "salty." In other words, if they become proud and unmerciful, they will be like salt that has lost its flavor and their opportunity to represent the Kingdom will be wasted.

QUESTIONS:

1. Through the followers of Jesus, the world gets a taste of the _____ of God.

2. Disciples bring the flavor of _____ and peace to a world made bitter by sin.

3. True or false: A person who is proud and unmerciful is being "salty."

4. True or false: "You are the salt of the earth" is an example of a metaphor.

5. True or false: The pure in heart will see God and dwell in His presence for all eternity (lesson 92).

6. In order to become poor in spirit, you must see yourself as

    (a) a sinner in need of God's mercy

    (b) a basically good person

    (c) always right about everything

Answers on page 181.

LESSON 96

LIGHT OF THE WORLD

MATTHEW 5:14-16

In the Bible, light is a symbol of holiness, goodness, and truth. Darkness is a symbol of sin, evil, and separation from God. Jesus says those who belong to the Kingdom of God bring the light of God's goodness and holiness to a world stumbling in the darkness of sin.

Jesus' disciples let their light shine through the things they do and say. They do good works—not to be praised by others, but so that others may see the goodness of God and give praise to Him.

The poor in spirit, the merciful, and the peacemakers are the salt of the earth and light of the world. Why? Because they are a lot like Jesus.

QUESTIONS:

1. True or false: In the Bible, light is a symbol of holiness, goodness, and truth.

2. How do Jesus' disciples let their light shine?

3. True or false: The poor in spirit do their good works in order to be praised by others.

4. Jesus said, "Let your _____ shine before men."

5. Disciples bring the flavor of _____ and peace to a world made bitter by sin (lesson 95).

6. True or false: A disciple of Jesus shows the goodness of God to others.

Answers on page 182.

LESSON 97

JESUS LOVES GOD'S LAW

MATTHEW 5:17-19; PSALM 40:8; PSALM 119:1-2, 97

The Pharisees thought they could get to Heaven by keeping God's Law, but they had actually set aside the Law of God for their own traditions. They did not delight to do God's will—they delighted to be seen and praised by others.

Jesus was not like them. He loved God's commandments. "Whoever obeys them and teaches others to do so will be called great in the kingdom of heaven," he said. He spent time thinking deeply about what God had said in His Law. He saw the Law and the rest of the Old Testament Scriptures as the very words of God, and that is why he cared so much about them.

In the end, it was the Law Jesus loved that made it necessary for him to die, not because he ever broke it, but because everyone else had—including you and me.

QUESTIONS:

1. The Pharisees had set aside the Law of God for their own _____ .

2. True or false: Jesus was a lot like the Pharisees.

3. Jesus saw the Law and the rest of the Old Testament as the _____ of God.

4. Jesus died because

    (a) he broke the Law

    (b) we broke the Law

    (c) no one broke the Law

5. The Pharisees thought they could get to Heaven by keeping the _____ .

6. True or false: Jesus loved God's Law.

Answers on page 182.

LESSON 98

LOVING YOUR ENEMIES

MATTHEW 5:43-48; LEVITICUS 19:17-18; ROMANS 2:4

Jesus is determined that we become like our heavenly Father if we are indeed His children. One way we can be more like God is by showing love and mercy to our enemies. In fact, this is what God does every day. He shows goodness and mercy to His enemies—those who rebel against Him and refuse to love His Son.

We must bless those who hurt us and pray for them remembering this is what Jesus did, and that it is the goodness of God that leads his enemies to repentance.

Loving our enemies will make us salt and light in a dark and bitter world. Loving our enemies will show that we are indeed sons of our Father in Heaven.

QUESTIONS:

1. Loving our _____ will show that we are sons of our Father in Heaven.
2. It is the
    (a) goodness
    (b) Law
    (c) anger
    of God that leads people to repentance.
3. True or false: We can be like the Father by showing love and mercy to our enemies.
4. Jesus died because
    (a) he broke the Law
    (b) we broke the Law
    (c) no one broke the Law
5. True or false: Jesus said, "Love your enemies and pray for those who persecute you."
6. Jesus loved God's _____ .

Answers on page 182.

116

LESSON 99

GIVING, PRAYING, AND FASTING

MATTHEW 6:1-4, 5-6, 16-18

We learned in lesson 85 that God looks into our hearts. That means He cares about *why* we do what we do. He knows if we do good things to be praised by others or if we do good things to bring praise to Him.

The Pharisees wanted to be seen and praised for everything they did. They wanted everyone to think well of them. Jesus said to the disciples, "Do not be like them" (Matthew 6:8). Instead, the disciples' good works were to be done from an attitude of love and obedience to their heavenly Father.

According to Jesus, the only works God will reward are the ones we do for His glory and the good of others.

QUESTIONS:

1. True or false: Some people do good things to be praised by others.

2. The Pharisees wanted to be _____ and praised for everything they did.

3. Jesus said, "Do not be _____ ."

4. True or false: God does not care about why we do what we do.

5. It is the

    (a) goodness

    (b) Law

    (c) anger

    of God that leads people to repentance.

6. True or false: According to Jesus, the only works God will reward are the ones we do for His glory and the good of others.

Answers on page 182.

LESSON 100

REAL TREASURE

MATTHEW 6:19-21; JOHN 8:29

Jesus Christ did not come to this world to get rich and famous. He didn't come to be a superstar or a president. He came to please his Father. His whole life was a life of loving his heavenly Father and doing His will. "I always do those things that please him," Jesus said. In this way, Jesus taught us how to lay up treasure—real treasure—in Heaven. We do this by living in a way that is pleasing to God.

A person that is devoted to pleasing the Father does not need to be afraid of thieves or moths or rust because his treasure is in Heaven—not in his closet or bank account. Unlike earthly treasures—things we can buy or build—heavenly treasure lasts forever and brings much more joy than money or fame.

QUESTIONS:

1. True or false: Jesus came into the world to get rich and famous.

2. Jesus said, "I always do those things that _____ Him."

3. Laying up treasure in Heaven means

    (a) being famous

    (b) being rich

    (c) pleasing God

4. True or false: Earthly treasures do not last forever.

5. Loving our _____ will show that we are truly sons of our Father in Heaven (lesson 98).

6. True or false: Jesus said we should lay up treasures on earth.

Answers on page 183.

LESSON 101

A HEALTHY HEART

MATTHEW 6:22-23; PSALM 119:36-37

One rule of bike riding is to keep your eyes focused on where you want to go, not where you don't want to go. Why? Because your bike will always follow your eyes. In the same way, as we walk around, our bodies go where our eyes lead them, and our lives follow the leading of our hearts as well.

Someone with a healthy heart (or "eye" as Jesus put it) is a person who loves what Jesus loves. He cares about pleasing God and bringing praise to Him. Our words, choices, and actions will bring God praise when our hearts are focused on pleasing Him—not on pleasing ourselves.

Jesus is teaching us to make sure that the things we love are the things he loves, so our lives will be going in the right direction.

QUESTIONS:

1. If we love what Jesus loves, then our lives will be going in the _____ direction.

2. A healthy heart is focused on

   (a) pleasing God

   (b) money

   (c) what others think

3. True or false: Our words, choices, and actions will always follow what our hearts are focused on.

4. True or false: Jesus came to please the scribes and Pharisees.

5. "Where your _____ is, there your _____ will be also."

6. True or false: Jesus said to seek earthly treasures.

Answers on page 183.

LESSON 102

A DIVIDED HEART

MATTHEW 6:24; EXODUS 20:1-3

Have you ever tried to ride a skateboard and do jumping jacks at the same time? Hold your breath and blow out a candle? If you did, you wouldn't be very successful. That is how it is with serving God—we cannot worship God and something else at the same time. It is like trying to go in two opposite directions at once and Jesus says it just will not work.

If we try to live for God *and* for earthly treasures, there is going to be a problem. Instead of being joyfully and completely devoted to God, we will be miserable. According to Jesus, either God will rule over us or our possessions will rule over us.

Jesus may have been thinking about the first Commandment as he taught this. It says, "You shall have no other gods besides Me." God demands and deserves our whole heart, not a divided heart. That is why Jesus says, "You *cannot* serve God and money."

QUESTIONS:

1. True or false: A divided heart is joyfully devoted to God.
2. A person who tries to live for God and money will be
    (a) happy
    (b) peaceful
    (c) miserable
3. Jesus said, "You cannot serve God and _____ ."
4. True or false: Our words, choices, and actions will always follow what our hearts are focused on.
5. "Where your _____ is, there your _____ will be also" (lesson 100).
6. What is the first Commandment?

Answers on page 183.

120

LESSON 103

MAKE UP YOUR MIND TO TRUST GOD

MATTHEW 6:25-34

If God takes care of little things like birds, flowers, and grass, how much more will he take care of His own children? In the Scripture for this lesson, Jesus tells his disciples three times, "Do not worry." It's as if he is saying, "Wake up! Don't you know who your Father is? The entire world belongs to Him. He is more than able to provide for your needs."

According to Jesus, trusting God is not an option—it is a command. Real trust in God makes a disciple different from others. The Father is pleased when we trust Him for everything. So a disciple must make up his mind to trust God and remember these words: do not worry.

QUESTIONS:

1. Jesus said "Seek first the _____ ."
2. True or false: God does not know everything we need.
3. What command did Jesus repeat three times in today's passage?
4. True or false: Food and clothes are the most important things in life.
5. Someone with a "healthy heart" cares about

    (a) pleasing God

    (b) having lots of money

    (c) what all of his friends think

6. A person who tries to live for God and money will be

    (a) happy

    (b) peaceful

    (c) miserable

Answers on page 183.

LESSON 104

BE CAREFUL HOW YOU THINK OF OTHERS

MATTHEW 7:1-5; JAMES 2:12-13

We are all fault-finders by nature. It is so easy to look at others and point out what is not right about them. If we fall into this habit, it is because we have forgotten how many things are not right about ourselves.

Remember that those who are merciful will receive mercy. But if we find it easy and even fun to pass judgment on others, Jesus says we will receive that same kind of judgment—without mercy.

Instead of being a fault-finder, Jesus says to deal first with our own sins, and then we will be able to take the speck out of our brother's eye. We may even find that the speck we thought we saw is no longer there.

QUESTIONS:

1. Instead of being a fault-finder, Jesus says to deal first with our own _____ .
2. True or false: God will be merciful to us even if we are not merciful to others.
3. Jesus said, "First take the _____ out of your own eye" (lesson 65).
4. Taking a log out of your eye is an example of
    (a) hyperbole
    (b) metaphor
    (c) a parable (lesson 65)
5. True or false: A divided heart is joyfully devoted to God.
6. Jesus said to seek first the _____ and His righteousness (lesson 103).

Answers on page 184.

LESSON 105

ASKING FOR GOOD THINGS

MATTHEW 7:7-12

Jesus' teaching shows us what true righteousness looks like and how far short of it we fall. He shines the light of God's Law on our hearts and reveals to us our lack of love, our pride, and our failure to love what he loves. But in his grace, he gives hope and a remedy for our need. And though it will not be easy, the remedy is really quite simple.

Knowing that the Father wants us to bear His image—to be like Him—Jesus tells us to *ask* for the things we need. "Make me loving, make me merciful, help me to love what you love and hate what you hate," is what we should ask from the Father. Jesus says if we keep asking, keep seeking, and keep knocking, the Father will give these good gifts to us.

As we have seen so far, the Father is gracious beyond measure. He gives all He has—even His very own Son—and we could have no greater gift.

QUESTIONS:

1. Jesus says if we keep asking, keep seeking, and keep knocking, the Father will
   (a) not give His good gifts to us
   (b) give His good gifts to us

2. True or false: Jesus gives us hope and a remedy for our need.

3. What does Jesus' teaching reveal about ourselves?
   (a) our goodness
   (b) our love for God
   (c) our pridefulness

4. Jesus tells us to _____ for the things we need.

5. Instead of being a fault-finder, Jesus says to deal first with our own _____ .

Answers on page 184.

LESSON 106

THE GOLDEN RULE

MATTHEW 7:7-12; MICAH 6:8

How do you want others to treat you? Jesus says to treat them in that very same way. At home, at school, or wherever, this should be our Golden Rule. In fact, this rule sums up all that the Old Testament tells us about how to live.

Do we want to be loved? Let us love others. Do we like others to be generous to us? Let us be generous to others. Do we want to be treated with kindness? Then let us treat others the way we want to be treated. After all, this is the way the Father treats us.

QUESTIONS:

1. What is the Golden Rule?
2. Whatever you wish that others would do to you, do also _____ .
3. Why should we treat others with goodness and mercy?
4. What does Jesus' teaching show us about ourselves?
    (a) our goodness
    (b) our love for God
    (c) our pridefulness
5. Taking a log out of your eye is an example of
    (a) hyperbole
    (b) metaphor
    (c) a parable

Answers on page 184.

LESSON 107

TWO ROADS: CHOOSE WISELY

MATTHEW 7:13-14

Near the end of the Sermon on the Mount, Jesus gives us a choice. If we obey and follow him, we will be on the narrow road that, though difficult, will lead to eternal life. If we choose the easy way of living however we want, then the end of that road will not be good.

Jesus once told his disciples, "I am the way, and the truth, and the life. No one comes to the Father except through me" (John 14:6). This means that only one road leads to Heaven, and it is the one on which we follow Jesus. *He* is the way. Compared to everyone who has ever lived, only a few will walk that road, and even then it is only by grace.

QUESTIONS:

1. Jesus said, "I am the _____ , and the _____ , and the life."

2. True or false: Jesus taught that there are many ways to Heaven.

3. How many people find the way to eternal life?

    (a) most

    (b) few

    (c) all

4. True or false: The "easy way" is living how we want and not how Jesus says we should.

5. What is the Golden Rule?

6. Why should we treat others with goodness and mercy?

Answers on page 184.

LESSON 108

BEWARE OF DOGS

MATTHEW 7:15-20; ACTS 20:28-30

False teachers love ignorant people—people who don't understand the Bible. Jesus says these "teachers" are pretenders and they want to make his disciples believe things that are not true. He tells us to beware of these "wolves in sheep's clothing," and he also tells us how to spot them.

"You will recognize (know) them by their *fruits*," he says. Do they teach what Jesus taught, or something slightly different? Do the things they say agree with Scripture? Do they follow Jesus and obey him? Do they look like God's children? Are they poor in spirit, meek, merciful, and pure in heart? Look for these kinds of things—what Jesus called "fruit"—and you will not be led astray.

QUESTIONS:

1. False leaders and teachers want to

    (a) make people believe things that are not true

    (b) help people follow Jesus

2. True or false: Jesus says that false prophets are like wolves dressed as sheep.

3. Jesus said, "I am the _____ , and the _____ , and the life."

4. True or false: The "easy way" is living how we want and not how Jesus says we should.

5. Jesus said, "You cannot serve God and _____ " (lesson 102).

Answers on page 185.

LESSON 109

THE SCARIEST VERSE IN THE BIBLE

MATTHEW 7:21-23

When a person's name is said twice in the Bible, it is a sign of close relationship and emotion. Some Old Testament examples are, "Abraham, Abraham," "Absalom, Absalom," and "Moses, Moses." On the cross, Jesus cried out, "My God, my God." Jesus says on the Day of Judgment many will call out, "Lord, Lord," thinking they are in a right relationship with him. But they will be wrong.

They did many things in his name, but something was missing. He says only those who do "the will of my Father in Heaven" will enter the Kingdom. These people have done their own will and not the will of the Father. They say to Jesus, "Lord, Lord," but have not obeyed his teaching. To their great surprise and horror, he will answer, "I never knew you. Go away from me, you lawbreakers!" Sadly, those are the last words they will ever hear him say.

QUESTIONS:

1. Jesus said, "Not everyone who says to me, _____ , will enter the Kingdom of Heaven."

2. True or false: In the Bible, when a person's name is said twice, it is a sign of close relationship and emotion.

3. True or false: All those who think they are going to Heaven really will go there.

4. Who are the ones who will enter the Kingdom?

5. True or false: The Sermon on the Mount tells us about the Father's will.

6. Jesus said, "You cannot serve God and _____ ."

Answers on page 185.

127

LESSON 110

THE WISE MAN BUILT HIS HOUSE ON THE ROCK

MATTHEW 7:24-27

As Jesus ends the Sermon on the Mount, he again gives us two choices: to obey or disobey. He says the wise person will hear his words, take them seriously, and put them into practice. The foolish person will be happy with his own religion and his own ideas about what God will approve of, but his false hopes will be swept away by the storm of God's judgment.

Going to church or being baptized does not make me a disciple of Jesus. Hearing his words and putting them into practice does. Obedience to Jesus shows the true condition of my heart—how I really think and feel about him. It shows how much I care about doing the will of the Father.

Build your house—your life—using his plans and not your own. Pay attention to your heart attitude and not just your behavior. Follow Jesus so that when the Judgment comes, your house will stand.

QUESTIONS:

1. What does the house represent in Jesus' story of the two builders?
2. True or false: Jesus said, "Everyone who hears these words of mine and does them is like a wise man who built his house on rock."
3. What does a true disciple of Jesus do with what Jesus teaches?
4. True or false: I can be sure I am a disciple of Jesus if I go to church and am baptized.
5. Obedience to Jesus shows the true condition of my _____ .
6. Blessed are the
   (a) pure in heart
   (b) divided in heart
   (c) ones who know all the right answers

Answers on page 185.

PART VIII

JESUS THE SAVIOR (PASSION WEEK)

LESSON 111

THE TRANSFIGURATION

MATTHEW 16:13-17; MATTHEW 17:1-8

When Jesus' outward appearance was changed, or *transfigured*, it was a sight the disciples would never forget. Peter, James, and John were amazed as the radiant light of Christ's glory shined upon them. His clothes became dazzling white and his face lit up like the sun. Peter had already said, "You are the Christ, the Son of the living God." Now God Himself says from Heaven, "This is my one dear Son, in whom I take great delight. Listen to him!"

Here on the mountain, Jesus was lifted up in brilliant glory. But soon, he would be lifted up on a cruel Roman cross.

QUESTIONS:

1. True or false: The disciples fell asleep when they saw Jesus transfigured.

2. What did Jesus look like when he was transfigured?

3. To *transfigure* means

   (a) to sail across the ocean

   (b) to change the outward appearance

   (c) to solve math problems

4. On the mountain, Jesus was lifted up in brilliant _____ .

5. The voice from Heaven said, "This is my _____ . Listen to him!"

6. True or false: Obedience to Jesus shows the true condition of my heart (lesson 110).

Answers on page 185.

LESSON 112

THE BEGINNING OF THE END

LUKE 9:51; ZECHARIAH 9:9

We learned in our very first lessons that Jesus was sent by God on a rescue mission. He came to rescue his people from their sins. And not long after raising Lazarus, Jesus went to Jerusalem to finish that mission. You might say it was the beginning of the end for Jesus.

This time in Jerusalem was going to be the final week of Jesus' life and is known as *Passion Week*. The word *passion* comes from a Latin word that means "to suffer." It would be the hardest week of his life, but he knew it was his Father's will and that his Father would be with him. Earlier Jesus told his disciples, "I came to do the will of the one who sent me" (John 6:38), and though all the powers of evil were against him, nothing was going to stop him.

Amazingly, the prophet Zechariah wrote about this event in detail nearly 500 years before it happened.

QUESTIONS:

1. True or false: Jesus was sent by God the Father on a rescue mission.

2. What Old Testament prophet spoke of Jesus coming into Jerusalem on a donkey?

3. Jesus came to do

    (a) his own will

    (b) the will of the people

    (c) the will of God the Father

4. "When the days drew near for him to be taken up, Jesus set his face to go to
    _____ " (Luke 9:51).

5. True or false: The last week of Jesus' life is known as Spring Break.

6. The voice from Heaven said, "This is my _____ . Listen to him!"

Answers on page 186.

LESSON 113

HOSANNA TO THE KING

LUKE 19:11, 28-40; PSALM 118:25-26

Just as Zechariah had said, Jesus rode into Jerusalem on a donkey, and all the hopes and dreams of his followers came with him. They expected him to deliver them from the Romans and make Israel a great nation once again. You could feel the excitement as they cried out in praise from the Psalms, "Hosanna to the King of Israel!" *Hosanna* means "save" or "rescue."

Like the disciples, the crowds were sure that Jesus was about to set up an earthly kingdom. But Jesus had not come to save them from the Romans. He came to save them from their sin. This King did not come to wear a crown of gold. He came to wear a crown of thorns.

QUESTIONS:

1. The crowds expected Jesus to deliver them from the _____ .

2. True or false: *Hosanna* means "save" or "rescue."

3. True or false: Many people thought Jesus would set up a kingdom on earth.

4. Jesus came to do the will of

   (a) God

   (b) the people

   (c) the Pharisees

5. On the mountain, Jesus was lifted up in brilliant _____ (lesson 111).

Answers on page 186.

LESSON 114

HIS HOUR HAD COME

JOHN 12:20-27

From the beginning of Jesus' ministry until he entered Jerusalem, he was always saying, "My time has not yet come." But now his time *had* come, and the time for him to lay down his life was at hand. Jesus saw his life as a grain of wheat that had to die in order to bring more fruit. He knew that only by his death would people be able to have eternal life.

Jesus also used the grain of wheat to teach his disciples more about what it means to follow him. He said it would mean a kind of dying—dying to selfish ways, and surrendering to the will of the Father. Only then will the disciple bear fruit that brings glory to his Lord.

QUESTIONS:

1. True or false: Jesus said, "Unless a grain of wheat falls to the ground and dies, it remains alone; but if it dies, it bears much fruit."

2. Jesus knew that only by his death would people be able to have _____ .

3. For a true disciple, following Jesus means

    (a) getting rich

    (b) having an easy life

    (c) dying to selfish ways

4. The crowds expected Jesus to deliver them from the _____ .

5. What Old Testament prophet spoke of Jesus coming into Jerusalem on a donkey (lesson 113)?

6. True or false: *Hosanna* means "save" or "rescue."

Answers on page 186.

LESSON 115

JESUS CLEANSES THE TEMPLE

MARK 11:15-18

Jesus loved his Father and he loved his Father's house. So when he saw the Temple in Jerusalem being used as a place for greedy men to make money, it was more than he could take. In holy anger, he overturned all the tables and sent doves and coins flying everywhere. Then, using the words of Isaiah and Jeremiah, he said, "It is written, My house will be called a house of prayer...but you have turned it into a den of robbers!"

The Temple was the place where God was to be worshiped—not money. What Jesus did was meant to bring the people to repentance and turn them back to God. And maybe it did for some, but not for all.

QUESTIONS:

1. Jesus loved his Father and he loved his Father's _____ .

2. True or false: The Temple in Jerusalem was where the people were to worship God.

3. What two Old Testament prophets did Jesus quote when he cleansed the Temple?

4. Jesus said, "My house will be called a house of _____ ."

5. Jesus wanted the people who were buying and selling in the Temple to

    (a) sell different items

    (b) ignore God

    (c) repent and worship God

6. What Old Testament prophet spoke of Jesus coming into Jerusalem on a donkey?

Answers on page 186.

LESSON 116

WHEN JESUS WAS ANGRY

MARK 11:15-18

Whenever we get angry, it is usually for selfish and sinful reasons. Things don't go the way we would like, or we don't get something we want. But what about Jesus? Was it sinful when he caused chaos in the Temple? The answer is no, and here is why.

Jesus was angry for the right reasons that day. His Father's house was being misused by greedy men and God was being dishonored. This stirred the heart of Jesus to anger; but even in his anger, he wanted to bring the people to repentance.

Yes, sometimes Jesus was angry, but it was always holy and righteous anger. Even then, he never sinned.

QUESTIONS:

1. Whenever we become angry, it is usually for the
   (a) right reasons
   (b) wrong reasons
   (c) glory of God

2. True or false: Jesus was angry for the right reasons.

3. True or false: Jesus never sinned.

4. Why do we often become angry?

5. What two Old Testament prophets did Jesus quote when he cleansed the Temple (lesson 115)?

6. Jesus wanted the people who were buying and selling in the Temple to
   (a) sell different items
   (b) ignore God
   (c) repent and worship God

Answers on page 187.

LESSON 117

THE UPPER ROOM

LUKE 22:7-15

Some of the most beloved things Jesus did and said were on the last night of his life in a place known as the Upper Room. It was there that he washed his disciples' feet, ate his final Passover meal, comforted his disciples, and taught them about the Holy Spirit.

The Upper Room was one of the last stops on his way to the cross. In our next few lessons, we will spend some time of our own in the Upper Room with the Lord and his dear disciples.

QUESTIONS:

1. True or false: On the last night of his life, Jesus taught his disciples in the Upper Room.
2. Name two things Jesus did in the Upper Room.
3. The Upper Room was one of the last stops on his way to the _____ .
4. Jesus said, "My house will be called a house of _____ ."
5. Jesus got angry for
    (a) the right reasons
    (b) the wrong reasons
    (c) no reason at all

Answers on page 187.

LESSON 118

THE PASSOVER MEAL

LUKE 22:14-15; EXODUS 12

The Passover meal was a reminder for the Jews of how God rescued them from slavery in Egypt. The night God brought death and judgment upon the land, they marked their doors with the blood of a lamb. God said, "When I see the blood I will pass over you" (Exodus 12:13). That is why it is called *Passover*—because God's judgment passed over His people.

Jesus used his last Passover meal to teach the disciples that God was about to rescue them from a different kind of slavery. Jesus himself would be the final Passover Lamb.

QUESTIONS:

1. True or false: The Passover meal was a reminder for the Jews of how God rescued them from slavery in Egypt.

2. The Israelites marked their houses with the _____ of a lamb.

3. God said, "When I see the _____ , I will pass over you."

4. Where did Jesus celebrate his last Passover meal?

5. True or false: Jesus used this meal to teach the disciples that God was about to rescue them from a different kind of slavery.

6. _____ was the final Passover Lamb.

Answers on page 187.

138

LESSON 119

THIS IS MY BODY

LUKE 22:14-19; ISAIAH 53:5

Jesus wanted his disciples to understand what he was about to do for them. So, as a living parable, he took the bread of the Passover meal and broke it, saying, "This is my body, which is given for you." It was as if he were saying to them, "Remember, I am the Bread of Life, and like this bread, I am about to be broken for you."

Jesus was going to die a cruel death. He was going to suffer God's punishment against our sin so that all who trust in Jesus would never have to face that punishment. Just as the bread was broken, so Jesus was wounded for our transgressions and crushed for our iniquities. It was the only way.

QUESTIONS:

1. As Jesus took the bread, he _____ it.

2. True or false: Jesus was teaching his disciples that he was going to be "broken" under God's judgment.

3. Jesus was going to suffer God's punishment against _____ .

4. God said, "When I see

   (a) your good works

   (b) the blood

   (c) you going to church

   I will pass over you."

5. Jesus was wounded for our transgressions and _____ .

Answers on page 187.

LESSON 120

THE BLOOD OF THE LAMB

MATTHEW 26:26-28

In the Sermon on the Mount, Jesus said he came to fulfill the Law. Part of that Law said that in order for God's people to be forgiven, a lamb without spot or blemish (in perfect health) must be killed in their place. Its blood was to be sprinkled on the altar inside the Holy Place of the Tabernacle. Without this shedding of blood, there could be no forgiveness. Why? Because God is holy. He must always do what is right, and for God to do what is right, He has to punish sin.

So in order for God's people to be forgiven once and for all time, a very special Lamb had to die. Not an animal, but a man who was without spot or blemish—that is, without sin. Only Jesus could be that Lamb because he alone was without sin.

Far greater than the lambs of the Old Testament, the blood of Christ himself would be poured out for our forgiveness.

QUESTIONS:

1. God's Law said that in order for His people to be forgiven, a _____ without spot or blemish must be killed in their place.

2. True or false: The blood of the lamb had to be sprinkled on the altar inside the Holy Place.

3. Without the shedding of blood, there could be no _____ .

4. True or false: In order for God's people to be forgiven once and for all time, a very special Lamb had to die.

5. Why must God punish sin?

   (a) because He must always do what is right

   (b) because He wants to be unkind

   (c) because we think He should

6. God said, "When I see _____ , I will pass over you" (lesson 118).

Answers on page 188.

LESSON 121

THIS IS MY BLOOD

MATTHEW 26:26-28; 1 JOHN 1:9

During the Passover meal, Jesus took a cup, gave thanks to the Father, and told his disciples to drink from it. This was probably the third cup used during the meal and it is known as the "cup of redemption" or the "cup of salvation." Psalm 116:13 says, "I will lift up the cup of salvation and call on the name of the Lord" (NIV).

Jesus said the wine in the cup represented his blood that was about to be shed on the cross. It was his death that would make forgiveness possible. It is the blood of Christ that cleanses us from all sin.

QUESTIONS:

1. The cup Jesus took was called the cup of _____ .

2. True or false: The wine in the cup represented the blood of Christ.

3. Psalm 116:13 says, "I will lift up the cup of _____ and call on the name of the Lord."

4. Why must God punish sin?

    (a) because He must always do what is right

    (b) because He wants to be unkind

    (c) because we think He should

5. True or false: It is the blood of Christ that cleanses us from all sin.

6. Which Psalm speaks about the cup of salvation?

Answers on page 188.

LESSON 122

NOT AS TOUGH AS YOU THINK

MARK 14:26-31

In every crowd there is usually one person who speaks up more than the rest, and of the twelve disciples, Simon Peter was that person. He was full of zeal and boldness for sure, but he was not as tough as he thought. On the night of Jesus' arrest, Peter would see that when he depended on himself instead of Jesus he was frail and weak.

After the Passover meal, Jesus told Peter, "Tonight, you will deny that you even know me." Peter answered, "Never!" All the other disciples said the same. They thought more of themselves and their own strength than they should have. We all do. But Jesus knew their weakness and he loved them anyway. He had a good plan for his beloved disciples. He always does.

QUESTIONS:

1. Who said, "Even if I must die with you, I will never deny (leave) you?"
2. True or false: On the night of Jesus' arrest, Peter would see that when he depended on himself instead of Jesus he was frail and weak.
3. Although Jesus knew his disciples were weak, he _____ them anyway.
4. True or false: Peter was a quiet person who would think before he spoke.
5. True or false: It is the blood of Christ that cleanses us from all sin.
6. Which Psalm speaks about the cup of salvation?

Answers on page 188.

LESSON 123

BAD NEWS FOR THE DISCIPLES

JOHN 13:33-14:3

When things do not go the way we hope, the disappointment can be hard to take. The disciples had high hopes that Jesus would soon set up his earthly kingdom and deliver Israel from all their enemies. But Jesus had bad news for them. He was about to go away and there would be no earthly kingdom—at least not yet.

Instead, he said he was going to be with the Father. Now this was *not* what they had hoped for, and when they heard it they were very sad. It seems that Jesus was teaching them another big lesson: when disappointment comes, we must trust God for better things. And better things were just around the corner.

QUESTIONS:

1. True or false: The disciples hoped that Jesus would soon set up his earthly kingdom.

2. When Jesus said he was going away, the disciples were
    (a) excited
    (b) disappointed

3. Jesus said he was going to be with the _____ .

4. When disappointment comes, we must
    (a) get angry
    (b) trust God
    (c) think selfish thoughts

5. True or false: Peter was a quiet person who would think before he spoke.

Answers on page 188.

LESSON 124

GOOD NEWS FOR THE DISCIPLES

JOHN 14:15-18, 25-26

The bad news was that Jesus was going away. The good news was that the Holy Spirit was coming in his place. Just as Jesus had been with the disciples, now the Holy Spirit would be with them. "He resides with you and *will be in you*," Jesus said (John14:17).

The Father promised to send the Holy Spirit to help, comfort, teach, and guide the disciples and all who would come to know and trust in Jesus. The disciples had much work to do in the future, and they could never do what needed to be done in their own power. But by the power of the Holy Spirit, they would be able to accomplish the mission Jesus would give them. This was good news indeed.

QUESTIONS:

1. What bad news had Jesus given his disciples?
2. What good news did he give them?
3. True or false: The disciples could fulfill their mission without the power of the Holy Spirit.
4. Who promised to send the Holy Spirit?
5. The Holy Spirit comes to

    (a) help and comfort us

    (b) confuse us

    (c) keep us from thinking

6. True or false: The Holy Spirit is present with all who know and trust in Jesus.

Answers on page 189.

LESSON 125

DIRTY FEET

JOHN 13:1-17

"When a disciple is fully trained, he will be like his teacher," Jesus once said. Jesus wanted his disciples to be like him—humble and serving. So not only did he tell them how, he also showed them how.

Though Jesus was God and King, he humbled himself, knelt down, and washed the disciples' dirty feet. He did it joyfully and without complaining. He did it because he loved them. He did it though they did not deserve it.

This is how we show true love for one another, by humbly serving one another the way Jesus did when He washed his disciples' feet. "I have given you an example—you should do just as I have done for you."

QUESTIONS:

1. True or false: Jesus wanted his disciples to be like him.

2. Jesus said, "I have given you an _____ . You should do just as I have done for you."

3. Though Jesus was God, he

   (a) humbled himself

   (b) bragged about himself

   (c) made sure everyone liked him

4. True or false: The disciples could tell that Jesus did not want to touch their feet.

5. The Holy Spirit comes to

   (a) help and comfort us

   (b) confuse us

   (c) keep us from thinking

6. True or false: The Holy Spirit is present with all who know and trust in Jesus (lesson 124).

Answers on page 189.

LESSON 126

THE GARDEN

MATTHEW 26:30-36

Now, as the night grows darker and darker, Jesus leaves the Upper Room and makes his way to a garden called Gethsemane. The name *Gethsemane* means "oil press." It was a place where the oil was pressed out of the olives that grew there.

The place and its name were a picture of what was about to happen to Jesus. Like the olives, Jesus' very life was going to be pressed out of him. As he prayed, he could feel the end pressing in upon him, and his soul was filled with sorrow. The time had come to fulfill the mission. The cup he had to drink was ready. We will learn more about this in our next lesson.

QUESTIONS:

1. Where did Jesus go after he left the Upper Room?

2. True or false: *Gethsemane* means "olive plant."

3. What was Jesus doing in the garden?

4. As Jesus prayed in the garden, his soul was filled with _____ .

5. Jesus said, "I have given you an _____ . You should do just as I have done for you." (lesson 125).

6. True or false: The disciples could tell that Jesus did not want to touch their feet.

Answers on page 189.

LESSON 127

THE CUP

MATTHEW 26:36-44

Jesus had never prayed so hard in his life. As if he were drowning, his soul was completely overcome by sorrow and distress. But why? The answer is found in the *cup*: "Father, can this cup be taken away? Do I have to drink it?" he cried.

The cup that Jesus prayed about was a symbol of unspeakable pain and suffering. It was a cup overflowing with God's terrible wrath and anger against sin. Drinking from this cup meant being punished for the sins of the world as if he himself had committed them all. Worst of all, the cup meant that for the first time in all eternity he would be separated from his Father.

As Jesus stared into the bitter cup, he could see the cross. He knew what he had to do.

QUESTIONS:

1. The cup Jesus prayed about was a symbol of unspeakable pain and _____ .
2. The cup was filled with God's _____ .
3. True or false: Jesus would be punished for the sins of the world as if he himself had committed them all.
4. Drinking the cup meant that Jesus would be _____ from his Father.
5. True or false: *Gethsemane* means "oil press."
6. What was Jesus doing in the garden?

Answers on page 189.

147

LESSON 128

YOUR WILL BE DONE

MATTHEW 26:36-44; JOHN 15:13

With his face to the ground, Jesus prayed three times with all his might, "My Father, if possible, let this cup pass from me! Yet not what I will, but what you will." Jesus was laying down his life. He was surrendering his will to the Father. He gave himself to God's great purpose and plan. Why? Because of love.

Jesus loves his Father, and Jesus loves you and me. He knew the cross was his Father's will and plan. He knew it was for our forgiveness. Jesus really did come to do His Father's will, and without question, there is no greater love than the love of Jesus.

QUESTIONS:

1. How many times did Jesus pray for the cup to be taken from him?

    (a) once

    (b) twice

    (c) three times

2. True or false: Jesus gave himself to God's great purpose and plan.

3. True or false: Jesus said, "My will be done."

4. There is no greater love than the love of _____ .

5. The cup Jesus prayed about was a symbol of unspeakable pain and _____ .

6. True or false: Jesus would be punished for the sins of the world as if he himself had committed them all.

Answers on page 190.

LESSON 129

ISAIAH 53:7-8; MATTHEW 27:27-31

After praying in Gethsemane, Jesus was betrayed by Judas and arrested by Roman soldiers. He was then given to the High Priest and taken to Pontius Pilate, a Roman governor. Pilate and his men questioned Jesus. They mocked him, mistreated him, and finally decided his fate.

These events fulfilled a 700-year-old prophecy made by Isaiah: "He was oppressed and afflicted...he was led like a lamb to the slaughter" (Isaiah 53:7, NIV). The gospel of Matthew says they led him away to crucify him. Jesus was taken to a place outside the city of Jerusalem called Golgotha, and there he was nailed to a wooden cross.

Jesus was being put to death for sins he did not commit. He had taken the cup, and it was the darkest moment in all of history.

QUESTIONS:

1. Jesus was led like a _____ to the slaughter.
2. True or false: Isaiah's 700-year-old prophecy was being fulfilled in Jesus.
3. There is no greater love than the love of _____ .
4. True or false: Jesus gave himself to God's great purpose and plan.
5. True or false: Jesus would be punished for the sins of the world as if he himself had committed them all.

Answers on page 190.

LESSON 130

THE SINS OF THE WORLD

ISAIAH 53:6; LEVITICUS 16:20-22; PSALM 103:12

Once a year the Jews observed a special day called the Day of Atonement. On that day, a goat was brought to the High Priest who stood with both hands upon the goat's head and confessed all the sins of Israel. Then the goat was led away to the desert and released, "carrying" all of those sins upon his head. The goat would wander away never be seen again.

On the cross, Jesus took all of our sins upon himself. Like the goat, he carried them away to the grave so that we could be forgiven and acceptable to God. And the sins Jesus takes away will never be seen again.

QUESTIONS:

1. What did the High Priest do to the goat?

2. The goat carried the _____ of Israel upon his head.

3. _____ took all of our sins upon himself.

4. True or false: Our guilt and sin was placed upon Jesus, though he had never sinned.

5. Jesus carried our sins away so we could

   (a) keep the Law

   (b) be forgiven

   (c) work our way to Heaven

6. What special day did the Jews observe once a year?

Answers on page 190.

150

LESSON 131

FORSAKEN BY GOD

ISAIAH 53:8; PSALM 22:1; MATTHEW 27:32-46

Just like the goat was separated from the people and from God, so Jesus with all our sin was separated from the Father. This is the greatest mystery in all of Scripture—that God could be somehow separated from God. In a way we will never fully understand, all of God's wrath and anger against our sin was poured out upon His Son on the cross.

This was the awful meaning of the cup. The Father was no longer with Jesus. Instead, because of our sin, He was against Jesus. In that moment, Jesus felt the full force of sin, darkness, holy wrath, and being left completely alone. Therefore from Psalm 22, he cried out, "My God, my God! Why have you forsaken me?"

QUESTIONS:

1. On the cross, Jesus was separated from _____ .

2. True or false: All of God's wrath and anger against our sin was poured out upon His Son on the cross.

3. _____ took all of our sins upon himself.

4. What Psalm did Jesus quote as he suffered on the cross?

5. Jesus carried our sins away so we could

   (a) keep the Law

   (b) be forgiven

   (c) work our way to Heaven

6. What special day did the Jews observe once a year (lesson 130)?

Answers on page 190.

151

LESSON 132

PAID IN FULL

ISAIAH 53:10-12; JOHN 19:28-30

After crying out, "Why have you forsaken me?" Jesus said, "It is finished." This meant that his mission was finally complete. The will of his Father had been done. He had taken the cup and there was nothing left in it.

Because of the evil in us, we could never be good enough for God to love or forgive us. We could never earn God's forgiveness by keeping a set of rules. He is too holy and we are too sinful.

But God demonstrated His love for people by giving His only Son to pay the penalty for our sin. Our sins were so many and the price was so high, we could never begin to pay what we owed to God. Instead, Jesus our Savior laid down his life and paid it all for us. So with the words, "It is finished," he bowed his head and died. Our sin debt was *paid in full*.

QUESTIONS:

1. True or false: When Jesus said, "It is finished," it meant that his mission was complete.

2. True or false: On the cross, all of God's wrath and anger against our sin was poured out upon His Son.

3. God demonstrated His love by giving His only Son to pay the penalty for our _____ .

4. True or false: We cannot earn God's forgiveness because He is too holy and we are too sinful.

5. On the cross, Jesus was separated from _____ (lesson 131).

6. True or false: Jesus gave himself to God's great purpose and plan.

Answers on page 191.

152

LESSON 133

OUR SUBSTITUTE

ISAIAH 53:5-6; EPHESIANS 5:2

In lesson 12 we learned that the words *for us* may be the most important words in the entire Bible. That is what a substitute is: one thing in place of another or one person in the place of another. Jesus did not deserve the cross—we did. But he went there *for us*, as our substitute. Jesus did not deserve punishment—we did. But he took our punishment *for us*.

The prophet Isaiah said that Jesus was pierced for our transgressions; he was crushed for our iniquities. He stood in our place and received our judgment from God. As we think about Jesus dying on the cross, keep in mind that he died for you and for me—in your place and mine.

Jesus is our only Substitute. He is the only one we will ever need.

QUESTIONS:

1. Jesus went to the cross for us, as our _____ .

2. What prophet said that Jesus was "crushed for our iniquities?"

3. Jesus stood in our place and received our

    (a) blessing from God

    (b) judgment from God

4. What Psalm did Jesus quote as he suffered on the cross (lesson 131)?

5. True or false: When Jesus said, "It is finished," it meant that his mission was complete and our debt to God was paid in full.

6. God demonstrated His love by giving His only Son to pay the penalty for our _____ (lesson 132).

Answers on page 191.

LESSON 134

NO SUBSTITUTE FOR JESUS

GALATIANS 2:15-16, 20-21; ACTS 4:10-12

Doing special work around the house is a great way to earn money. It is known as working for an allowance. However, God's forgiveness can never be earned. All the good works we could ever do would never be able to meet the demands of His holy Law.

The good news is that we do not have to earn forgiveness because Jesus has done all that needs to be done for us. His life and death given on our behalf is the only thing God will accept for our salvation. He *alone* is our Substitute. If we try to substitute our works for Jesus' works or add anything to what he has done, we are saying to God that Jesus is not good enough, and nothing could be more offensive to God. There is simply no other way to the Father but through trusting in the finished work of His Son.

QUESTIONS:

1. True or false: We can earn God's forgiveness by doing good works.

2. All of our works could never meet the demands of God's _____ .

3. To say that Jesus is not good enough is

    (a) right

    (b) pleasing to God

    (c) offensive to God

4. What Psalm did Jesus quote as he suffered on the cross (lesson 131)?

5. True or false: When Jesus said, "It is finished," it meant that his mission was complete and our debt to God was paid in full.

6. Jesus stood in our place and received our

    (a) blessing from God

    (b) judgment from God

Answers on page 191.

LESSON 135

RAISED ON THE THIRD DAY

1 CORINTHIANS 15:3-8; LUKE 24:1-9

When Neil Armstrong became the first man to walk on the moon, he received a standing ovation because he had accomplished an amazing mission. When Jesus accomplished his mission, God the Father gave him something far greater: he raised Jesus to life. Scripture says, "Christ was raised from the dead through the glory (power) of the Father" (Romans 6:4).

Christ's resurrection meant that death had been defeated. Sin had been crushed. The Father had accepted his life as the final sacrifice for sin. Jesus rose as a victorious Savior and his resurrection is the key to the hope of every believer. Without the resurrection, faith in Christ would be worthless and we would be hopeless.

But the reality is that Christ *did* rise from the dead. He is risen. He is risen indeed.

QUESTIONS:

1. When Jesus accomplished his mission, _____ raised him from the dead.
2. Scripture says, "Christ was raised from the dead through the _____ of the Father."
3. What did Christ's resurrection mean?
4. True or false: Without the resurrection, faith in Christ would be worthless.
5. On the _____ day, Christ rose from the dead.
6. All of our works could never meet the demands of God's _____ (lesson 134).

Answers on page 191.

LESSON 136

JESUS APPEARS TO THE DISCIPLES

LUKE 24:36-53

After the resurrection Jesus appeared to many different people. He appeared to the women at the tomb, he appeared to Peter and the rest of the disciples, and then he appeared to more than 500 others. They could see with their own eyes that it was the Lord. They touched his hands and his feet and were amazed. Sometimes, he even ate with them.

On these occasions, Jesus opened the Old Testament and showed them everything that was written about him there. He gave them understanding and assurance that the Scriptures concerning him had been fulfilled. As they heard these things, the disciples were filled with joy—so much joy that they spent the rest of their lives telling the story.

QUESTIONS:

1. When Jesus rose from the dead, he appeared to
   (a) the Pharisees
   (b) Peter and many others

2. How many people saw Jesus after the resurrection?

3. The disciples touched Jesus' _____ and his _____ .

4. True or false: The Old Testament Scriptures concerning Jesus were fulfilled.

5. True or false: Without the resurrection, faith in Christ would be worthless.

6. Scripture says, "Christ was raised from the dead through the _____ of the Father" (lesson 135).

Answers on page 192.

156

LESSON 137

WORK TO BE DONE

MATTHEW 28:18-20; LUKE 24:44-49; ACTS 1:8

Jesus not only gave his disciples understanding about all that had happened—he gave them a mission. He sent them out to preach his message of repentance and forgiveness of sins. They were to go and make disciples from every nation, beginning in Jerusalem and then to the ends of the earth.

But how could they possibly carry out such a task? By the same power that Jesus had: "Behold, I am sending the promise of my Father upon you, and you will be clothed with power from on high," Jesus told them. "You will receive power when the Holy Spirit has come upon you, and you will be my witnesses in Jerusalem, and in all Judea and Samaria, and to the farthest parts of the earth."

It was the power of God the Holy Spirit that would fill them and give their work success.

QUESTIONS:

1. True or false: Jesus gave his disciples a mission to preach the gospel.

2. Jesus said, "Go and make _____ of all nations."

3. What was the promise of the Father (lesson 124)?

4. How would the disciples be able to succeed in the mission Jesus gave them?

   (a) by their own strength

   (b) by eating a good breakfast

   (c) by the power of the Holy Spirit

5. True or false: Without the resurrection, faith in Christ would be worthless.

6. How many others saw Jesus after his resurrection (lesson 136)?

Answers on page 192.

LESSON 138

TAKEN UP, BUT COMING AGAIN

ACTS 1:1-11; MATTHEW 24:30-31, 36-44

Jesus had told the disciples that he was going back to the Father, and now that time had come. In utter amazement, they gazed into Heaven as their Master was taken up from them. With his promises still ringing in their ears, he disappeared out of sight.

Suddenly, two angels appeared in the form of men and gave them this assurance: Jesus would come again in the same way as they saw him go. No doubt the disciples remembered Jesus say, "The Son of Man will come on the clouds of Heaven with power and great glory...be working...be watching...be ready" (Matthew 25).

With these words of the Lord Jesus Christ, we come to our final lesson. But the journey of seeing the glory and power of Christ is not over. There is so much more to be discovered about Jesus, and if you continue to explore his life, he will provide for you a lifetime of learning. Jesus is far greater than we could ever imagine, and I hope that you will come to know and love him above all other things.

So, as we continue our journey with Christ and wait eagerly for his return, may his words never stop ringing in our ears: "...be working...be watching...be ready."

QUESTIONS:

1. True or false: The disciples and others saw Jesus taken up into Heaven.
2. Who appeared as Jesus went out of sight?
3. The angels said Jesus would _____ in the same way they saw him go.
4. How many others saw Jesus after the resurrection (lesson 136)?
5. Jesus gave his disciples a mission to preach

   (a) nice stories

   (b) the latest news

   (c) the message about Jesus and what he had done

6. It was the power of the _____ that would fill the disciples and give their work success (lesson 137).

Answers on page 192.

ANSWER KEY

LESSON ONE

1. God
2. Son
3. Bible

LESSON TWO

1. c) as a baby boy
2. true
3. Mary
4. true

LESSON THREE

1. "God with us"
2. He was God.
3. true
4. c) as a baby boy

LESSON FOUR

1. "God with us"
2. "the LORD saves"
3. God
4. b) on a rescue mission

LESSON FIVE

1. Egypt
2. rescue
3. They were slaves of (or to) sin.
4. c) a slave to sin
5. Jesus

LESSON SIX

1. Bethlehem
2. a) Nazareth
3. He needed to become a servant.
4. sins
5. "house of bread"

LESSON SEVEN

1. to read, write, and count
2. the Old Testament
3. Nazareth
4. Jesus' earthly father, a carpenter

LESSON EIGHT

1. wisdom, increased
2. the Temple
3. c) listening to the teachers and asking them questions
4. yes

LESSON NINE

1. true
2. John the Baptist
3. Jesus
4. true

LESSON TEN

1. Pharisees
2. laws
3. false
4. they were blinded by their sin
5. Jesus

LESSON ELEVEN

1. 30
2. God the Father
3. "This is my one dear Son; in him I take great delight."
4. true
5. true

LESSON TWELVE

1. for us
2. a) for us
3. true
4. true
5. die

LESSON 13

1. "You are my one dear Son; in you I take great delight."
2. love
3. gave up
4. true

LESSON 14

1. Holy Spirit
2. true
3. ministry
4. in

LESSON 15

1. Satan (the devil)
2. true
3. false
4. with, in

LESSON 16

1. nothing
2. forty days
3. no
4. full

LESSON 17

1. c) by using the sword of the Spirit (the Scriptures)
2. true
3. the Scriptures
4. false

LESSON 18

1. God
2. by using the Scripture
3. three, Deuteronomy
4. false

LESSON 19

1. forty days
2. will
3. true
4. false

LESSON 20

1. Jesus showed his trust by his obedience.
2. true
3. the will of God
4. the Scriptures
5. b) the book of Deuteronomy

LESSON 21

1. He wanted Jesus to bow down and worship him.
2. kingdoms of the world
3. false
4. Deuteronomy
5. obedience and faithfulness to God

LESSON 22

1. full of grace and truth
2. three years
3. Gospel
4. true
5. the Holy Spirit

LESSON 23

1. untouchable
2. no
3. true
4. "the LORD saves"
5. "God with us"

LESSON 24

1. true
2. false
3. "Those who are healthy don't need a physician, but those who are sick do."
4. embarrassed
5. grace, truth

LESSON 25

1. "Daughter, your faith has made you well. Go in peace."
2. c) He spoke gently to her and healed her disease
3. false
4. the Holy Spirit

LESSON 26

1. true
2. truth, Father
3. truth
4. c) know and worship God

LESSON 27

1. "truly, truly I say to you"
2. "This is my one dear Son. Listen to him!"
3. a) know and worship God
4. true

LESSON 28

1. way, truth, life
2. b) only one
3. true
4. "truly, truly I say to you"
5. false

LESSON 29

1. praise from God
2. false
3. people
4. b) sinful people
5. Martha, Lazarus, Mary

LESSON 30

1. about 30 years old (Luke 3:23)
2. about three years
3. true
4. follow him
5. false

LESSON 31

1. Isaiah 61
2. true
3. fulfilled
4. Jesus
5. false, they were amazed at his words

LESSON 32

1. no
2. false
3. no
4. truth
5. b) Isaiah (chapter 61)
6. someone who is not a Jew

LESSON 33

1. a) Capernaum
2. Capernaum means "village of Nahum"
3. true
4. cliff
5. someone who is not Jewish

LESSON 34

1. Jesus went into Galilee, proclaiming the good news.
2. Kingdom of Heaven
3. false
4. The Kingdom of God
5. true

LESSON 35

1. people
2. Simon, Andrew, James, John
3. twelve
4. Apostles
5. the message of the Kingdom of Heaven

LESSON 36

1. disciples
2. c) learner
3. false, by following him and learning from him
4. follow me
5. like

LESSON 37

1. d) waste time
2. his miracles of healing
3. true
4. follow me
5. like

LESSON 38

1. so Jesus could heal his legs
2. sins
3. false
4. Kingdom
5. c) fishers of men

LESSON 39

1. because Jesus was claiming to be God
2. God
3. true
4. God
5. c) God with us

LESSON 40

1. "Get up, take up your mat and go home."
2. false
3. words
4. c) filled with awe
5. true

LESSON 41

1. God
2. hearts
3. "Your sins are forgiven."
4. God
5. thoughts
6. false

LESSON 42

1. true
2. glory
3. in his working great miracles
4. d) the glory of Christ
5. sinful people
6. Kingdom of Heaven

LESSON 43

1. c) the Son of God
2. about thirty-four
3. nature, sickness, demons, and even death
4. false
5. true
6. glory

LESSON 44

1. devil
2. b) pigs
3. true
4. Jesus came to his rescue
5. because he was filled with the Holy Spirit and with power
6. true

LESSON 45

1. true
2. false
3. angry
4. healed
5. Immanuel

LESSON 46

1. true
2. c) excited
3. faith
4. "Son of David, have mercy on me!"
5. sin
6. true

LESSON 47

1. "What kind of man is this?"
2. the Sea of Galilee
3. "Peace! Be still."
4. c) amazed
5. false
6. "Son of David, have mercy on me!"

LESSON 48

1. true
2. five thousand
3. bread
4. d) help us understand who he is
5. false

LESSON 49

1. He makes the sick well, gives the blind sight
2. faith
3. false
4. b) help us understand who he is
5. "What kind of man is this?"

LESSON 50

1. c) know and serve the God who made us
2. true
3. sin in us
4. faith
5. true

LESSON 51

1. Jairus
2. true
3. "Little girl, get up!"
4. death
5. faith, trust

LESSON 52

1. "pleasant"
2. c) stopped and cared for her himself
3. true
4. dead
5. "Young man, I say to you, get up!"

LESSON 53

1. true
2. b) slow to trust Jesus
3. God
4. c) the Bible
5. true
6. about 2000 years ago

LESSON 54

1. wake him up
2. he wakes the dead
3. Jairus' little girl, the widow's son, Lazarus
4. c) dead in sin
5. the Bible
6. God

LESSON 55

1. Jesus
2. b) eternal life
3. true
4. Resurrection, Life

LESSON 56

1. four days
2. thanks
3. by calling him out with a loud voice
4. false
5. grave
6. true

LESSON 57

1. false
2. faith
3. b) missed out on many blessings
4. true
5. Resurrection
6. true

LESSON 58

1. think, feel
2. true
3. b) missed out on many blessings
4. false
5. true

LESSON 59

1. false
2. anyone who would listen
3. synagogues, seaside, open fields, countryside
4. "teacher"
5. true
6. a) teach others

LESSON 60

1. very words
2. true
3. false
4. wisdom
5. "teacher"
6. false, about 45 times

LESSON 61

1. true
2. faithful
3. God
4. wisdom
5. "teacher"
6. true

LESSON 62

1. grace
2. true
3. God
4. false
5. b) was kind to his students
6. synagogues, seaside, open fields, countryside

LESSON 63

1. true
2. overstatement, hyperbole, similes
3. true
4. false
5. God

LESSON 64

1. true
2. loyalty
3. b) love others
4. true

LESSON 65

1. c) hyperbole
2. true
3. people swallowing camels, camels fitting into the eye of a needle
4. true
5. c) exaggeration (something impossible)

LESSON 66

1. simile
2. tombs
3. on the outside they appeared to people to be righteous but on the inside were full of hypocrisy and wickedness
4. true
5. overstatement, simile, hyperbole

LESSON 67

1. true
2. false
3. "You are the light of the world" "I am the Bread of Life" "This is my body which is broken for you"
4. ferocious wolves
5. true

LESSON 68

1. Psalms, Proverbs, Prophets
2. true
3. b) easy to remember
4. true
5. to help people understand and remember what he taught

LESSON 69

1. true
2. treasure, heart
3. Psalms, Proverbs, Prophets
4. true
5. "Where your treasure is, there your heart will be also" "You cannot serve God and money" "Do not be anxious for tomorrow, for tomorrow will be anxious for itself"

LESSON 70

1. at least forty
2. true
3. seeds, coins, sheep
4. the Kingdom of God, the love of God the Father
5. true

LESSON 71

1. What is the main point of this parable?
2. true
3. a) a point
4. the Kingdom of God, the love of God the Father
5. true

LESSON 72

1. parables, situations
2. false
3. God loves sinners or to show the Pharisees how unlike the Father they were
4. the father and his two sons
5. grace

LESSON 73

1. the tax collectors and sinners
2. c) forgiveness
3. false
4. true
5. What is the main point of this parable?

LESSON 74

1. false
2. he ran to his son, threw his arms around him, and kissed him
3. false
4. a) right thing
5. What is the main point of this parable?

LESSON 75

1. c) how wrong they were
2. true
3. the Father
4. a) right thing
5. mercy

LESSON 76

1. false
2. Kingdom of God
3. true
4. good news
5. c) the Kingdom of God

LESSON 77

1. "Heaven"
2. true
3. true
4. Kingdom of God
5. God
6. true

LESSON 78

1. false
2. Isaiah
3. ending
4. Kingdom of God
5. c) the Kingdom of Heaven

LESSON 79

1. will
2. true
3. king and domain
4. true
5. will
6. beginning, ending

LESSON 80

1. "the will of my Father"
2. true
3. true
4. c) someone who does the will of God and seeks His glory
5. will
6. Isaiah

LESSON 81

1. not yet, or yet to come
2. false
3. future
4. c) someone who does the will of God and seeks His glory
5. "the will of my Father"

LESSON 82

1. Kingdom
2. time, Kingdom
3. true
4. b) repent and give ourselves to Jesus
5. false

LESSON 83

1. Kingdom
2. true
3. the Kingdom of God to come and His will be done
4. b) repent and give ourselves to Jesus
5. because of all the bad things that are a part of this world such as sin, suffering, disease, and death
6. Jesus

LESSON 84

1. the value of the Kingdom
2. all the money and things in the world
3. b) lots of joy
4. for God's will to be done and His Kingdom to come
5. true
6. because of all the bad things that are a part of this world such as sin, suffering, sickness, disease, and death
7. answers will vary

LESSON 85

1. true
2. they thought the Pharisees were very righteous
3. proud
4. Kingdom of Heaven
5. true
6. b) repent and give ourselves to Jesus

LESSON 86

1. true
2. righteousness or goodness
3. holy
4. true
5. in our thoughts, words, and deeds
6. a) happy

LESSON 87

1. Kingdom of Heaven
2. false
3. true
4. b) is not poor in spirit
5. holy like the Father
6. the gospel of Matthew chapters 5-7

LESSON 88

1. by the merciful and gracious forgiveness of the Father
2. worthy
3. false
4. God
5. b) is not poor in spirit
6. the gospel of Matthew chapters 5-7

LESSON 89

1. Psalm 37
2. patience
3. false
4. by the merciful and gracious forgiveness of the Father
5. mercy
6. Kingdom of Heaven

LESSON 90

1. food and water
2. a right relationship with God and a right relationship with others
3. false
4. filled or satisfied
5. will
6. b) is not poor in spirit

LESSON 91

1. true
2. b) forgiveness
3. they say hurtful things, do mean things, mistreat us
4. anger, love
5. false
6. filled or satisfied

LESSON 92

1. true
2. idol
3. Psalm 24
4. d) Christ alone
5. true
6. b) forgiveness

LESSON 93

1. true
2. image
3. c) seeking peace and blessing for others
4. children of God
5. idol
6. false

LESSON 94

1. Heaven
2. we may be made fun of, talked about, left out, and falsely accused of doing wrong
3. false
4. c) seeking peace and good for others
5. righteousness
6. Psalm 24

LESSON 95

1. goodness
2. mercy
3. false
4. true
5. true
6. a) as a sinner in need of God's mercy

LESSON 96

1. true
2. through the things they do and say
3. false
4. light
5. mercy
6. true

LESSON 97

1. traditions
2. false
3. very words
4. b) we broke the Law
5. Law of God
6. true

LESSON 98

1. enemies
2. a) goodness
3. true
4. b) we broke the Law
5. true
6. Law

LESSON 99

1. true
2. seen
3. like them
4. false
5. a) goodness
6. true

LESSON 100

1. false
2. please
3. c) pleasing God
4. true
5. enemies
6. false

LESSON 101

1. right
2. a) pleasing God
3. true
4. false
5. treasure, heart
6. false

LESSON 102

1. false
2. c) miserable
3. money
4. true
5. treasure, heart
6. "You shall have no other gods besides Me."

LESSON 103

1. Kingdom of God, righteousness
2. false
3. do not be anxious or worried
4. false
5. a) pleasing God
6. c) miserable

LESSON 104

1. sins
2. false
3. log or beam
4. a) hyperbole
5. false
6. Kingdom of God

LESSON 105

1. b) give His good gifts to us
2. true
3. c) our pridefulness
4. ask
5. sins

LESSON 106

1. to treat others the way we want to be treated
2. to them
3. because that is how the Father treats us
4. c) our pridefulness
5. a) hyperbole

LESSON 107

1. way, truth
2. false
3. b) few
4. true
5. to treat others the way we want to be treated
6. because that is how the Father treats us

LESSON 108

  1. a) make people believe things that are not true

  2. true

  3. way, truth

  4. true

  5. money

LESSON 109

  1. "Lord, Lord"

  2. true

  3. false

  4. "only those who do the will of my Father"

  5. true

  6. money

LESSON 110

  1. our lives, or how we live

  2. true

  3. hear his words, take them seriously, and put them into practice

  4. false

  5. heart

  6. a) pure in heart

LESSON 111

  1. false

  2. His clothes became dazzling white and his face lit up like the sun

  3. b) to change the outward appearance

  4. glory

  5. one dear Son

  6. true

LESSON 112

1. true
2. Zechariah
3. c) the will of God the Father
4. Jerusalem
5. false
6. one dear Son

LESSON 113

1. Romans
2. true
3. true
4. a) God
5. glory

LESSON 114

1. true
2. eternal life
3. c) dying to selfish ways
4. Romans
5. Zechariah
6. true

LESSON 115

1. house
2. true
3. Isaiah and Jeremiah
4. prayer
5. c) repent and worship God
6. Zechariah

LESSON 116

1. b) wrong reasons
2. true
3. true
4. because things don't go the way we would like, or we don't get something we want
5. Isaiah and Jeremiah
6. c) repent and worship God

LESSON 117

1. true
2. He washed his disciples' feet, ate his final Passover meal, comforted his disciples, and taught them about the Holy Spirit.
3. cross
4. prayer
5. a) the right reasons

LESSON 118

1. true
2. blood
3. blood
4. Upper Room
5. true
6. Jesus

LESSON 119

1. broke
2. true
3. our sin
4. b) the blood
5. crushed for our iniquities

LESSON 120

1. lamb
2. true
3. forgiveness of sin
4. true
5. a) because He must always do what is right
6. the blood

LESSON 121

1. redemption or salvation
2. true
3. salvation
4. a) because He must always do what is right
5. true
6. Psalm 116:13

LESSON 122

1. Peter
2. true
3. loved
4. false
5. true
6. Psalm 116:13

LESSON 123

1. true
2. b) disappointed
3. Father
4. b) trust God
5. false

LESSON 124

1. Jesus was going away
2. the Holy Spirit was coming in his place
3. false
4. the Father
5. a) help and comfort us
6. true

LESSON 125

1. true
2. example
3. a) humbled himself
4. false
5. a) help and comfort us
6. true

LESSON 126

1. a garden called Gethsemane
2. false, it means oil press
3. praying
4. sorrow
5. example
6. false

LESSON 127

1. suffering
2. terrible wrath and anger against sin
3. true
4. separated
5. true
6. praying

LESSON 128

1. c) three times
2. true
3. false
4. Jesus
5. suffering
6. true

LESSON 129

1. lamb
2. true
3. Jesus
4. true
5. true

LESSON 130

1. stood with both hands upon the goat's head and confessed all the sins of Israel
2. sins
3. Jesus
4. true
5. b) be forgiven
6. the Day of Atonement

LESSON 131

1. the Father
2. true
3. Jesus
4. Psalm 22:1
5. b) be forgiven
6. the Day of Atonement

LESSON 132

1. true
2. true
3. sin
4. true
5. the Father
6. true

LESSON 133

1. Substitute
2. Isaiah
3. b) judgment from God
4. Psalm 22:1
5. true
6. sin

LESSON 134

1. false
2. Law
3. c) offensive to God
4. Psalm 22:1
5. true
6. b) judgment from God

LESSON 135

1. God the Father
2. glory
3. death had been defeated and sin had been crushed, his sacrifice was accepted by the Father
4. true
5. third
6. Law

LESSON 136

1. b) Peter and many others
2. more than 500
3. hands, feet
4. true
5. true
6. glory

LESSON 137

1. true
2. disciples
3. to send the Holy Spirit
4. c) by the power of the Holy Spirit
5. true
6. more than 500

LESSON 138

1. true
2. two angels
3. come again, return
4. over 500
5. c) the message about Jesus and what he had done
6. Holy Spirit

CPSIA information can be obtained
at www.ICGtesting.com
Printed in the USA
BVHW062036130319
542570BV00001B/10/P